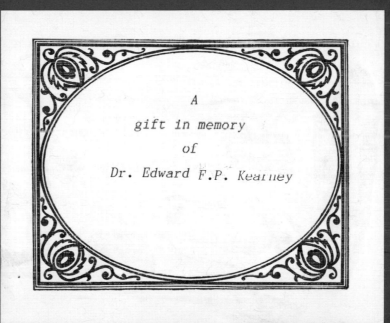

A
gift in memory
of
Dr. Edward F.P. Kearney

Fists of Steel

By the Editors of Time-Life Books

Alexandria, Virginia

TIME
LIFE ®

Time-Life Books Inc.
is a wholly owned subsidiary of

Time Incorporated

FOUNDER: Henry R. Luce 1898-1967
Editor-in-Chief: Jason McManus
Chairman and Chief Executive Officer:
J. Richard Munro
President and Chief Operating Officer:
N. J. Nicholas, Jr.
Editorial Director: Ray Cave
Executive Vice President, Books: Kelso F. Sutton
Vice President, Books: Paul V. McLaughlin

Time-Life Books Inc.

EDITOR: George Constable
Executive Editor: Ellen Phillips
Director of Design: Louis Klein
Director of Editorial Resources: Phyllis K. Wise
Editorial Board: Russell B. Adams, Jr., Dale M.
Brown, Roberta Conlan, Thomas H. Flaherty, Lee
Hassig, Donia Ann Steele, Rosalind Stubenberg
Director of Photography and Research:
John Conrad Weiser
Assistant Director of Editorial Resources:
Elise Ritter Gibson

PRESIDENT: Christopher T. Linen
Chief Operating Officer: John M. Fahey, Jr.
Senior Vice Presidents: Robert M. DeSena,
James L. Mercer, Paul R. Stewart
Vice Presidents: Stephen L. Bair, Ralph J. Cuomo,
Neal Goff, Stephen L. Goldstein, Juanita T. James,
Hallett Johnson III, Carol Kaplan, Susan J.
Maruyama, Robert H. Smith, Joseph J. Ward
Director of Production Services:
Robert J. Passantino
Supervisor of Quality Control: James King

The Cover: Formations of He 111 bombers
drone over Berlin on April 20, 1939, launching
a massive celebration of Adolf Hitler's
fiftieth birthday and the resurgence of
Germany as a military power.

This volume is one of a series that chronicles
the rise and eventual fall of Nazi Germany.

The Third Reich

SERIES DIRECTOR: Thomas H. Flaherty
Series Administrator: Norma E. Shaw
Editorial Staff for *Fists of Steel:*
Designer: Raymond Ripper
Picture Editor: Jane Jordan
Text Editors: John Newton, Henry Woodhead
Senior Writer: Stephen G. Hyslop
Researchers: Trudy Pearson (principal); Kirk E.
Denkler, Philip Brandt George, Philip M. Murphy,
Paula York-Soderlund
Assistant Designers: Alan Pitts, Tina Taylor
Copy Coordinator: Charles J. Hagner
Picture Coordinator: Robert H. Wooldridge
Editorial Assistant: Patricia D. Whiteford

Special Contributors: Ronald H. Bailey, Thomas
A. Lewis, Brian C. Pohanka, Moira J. Saucer,
David S. Thomson; Bryce Walker (text);
Jean Getlein, Marilyn Murphy (research);
Michael Kalen Smith (index)

Editorial Operations
Copy Chief: Diane Ullius
Production: Celia Beattie
Library: Louise D. Forstall

Correspondents: Elisabeth Kraemer-Singh
(Bonn); Christine Hinze (London); Maria
Vincenza Aloisi (Paris); Ann Natanson (Rome).
Valuable assistance was also provided by: Angie
Lemmer (Bonn); Brigid Grauman, Gay Kavanagh
(Brussels); Judy Aspinall, Linda Proud (London);
Trini Bandrés (Madrid); Elizabeth Brown,
Christina Lieberman (New York); Josephine
du Brusle (Paris).

First printing. Printed in U.S.A.

Published simultaneously in Canada.
School and library distribution by Silver Burdett
Company, Morristown, New Jersey 07960.

TIME-LIFE is a trademark of Time Incorporated
U.S.A.

**Library of Congress Cataloging in
Publication Data**
Fists of steel / by the editors of Time-Life Books.
   p.   cm. — (The Third Reich)
   Bibliography: p.
   Includes index.
   ISBN 0-8094-6966-9.
   ISBN 0-8094-6967-7 (lib. bdg.)
   1. Industrial mobilization—Germany—
History—20th century.   2. Spain—History—Civil
War, 1936-1939—Participation, German.
3. Spain. Ejército Nacional. Legión Cóndor.
I. Time-Life Books.   II. Series.
UA18.G4F57 1989   355.2'6—dc19   88-20071

Other Publications:

AMERICAN COUNTRY
VOYAGE THROUGH THE UNIVERSE
THE TIME-LIFE GARDENER'S GUIDE
MYSTERIES OF THE UNKNOWN
TIME FRAME
FIX IT YOURSELF
FITNESS, HEALTH & NUTRITION
SUCCESSFUL PARENTING
HEALTHY HOME COOKING
UNDERSTANDING COMPUTERS
LIBRARY OF NATIONS
THE ENCHANTED WORLD
THE KODAK LIBRARY OF CREATIVE PHOTOGRAPHY
GREAT MEALS IN MINUTES
THE CIVIL WAR
PLANET EARTH
COLLECTOR'S LIBRARY OF THE CIVIL WAR
THE EPIC OF FLIGHT
THE GOOD COOK
WORLD WAR II
HOME REPAIR AND IMPROVEMENT
THE OLD WEST

For information on and a full description of any
of the Time-Life Books series listed above, please
call 1-800-621-7026 or write:
Reader Information
Time-Life Customer Service
P.O. Box C-32068
Richmond, Virginia 23261-2068

General Consultants

Col. John R. Elting, USA (Ret.), former associate professor at West Point, has written or edited some twenty books, including *Swords around a Throne, The Superstrategists,* and *American Army Life,* as well as *Battles for Scandinavia* in the Time-Life Books World War II series. He was chief consultant to the Time-Life series, The Civil War.

George H. Stein, distinguished teaching professor of history at the State University of New York at Binghamton, received his Ph.D. in history from Columbia University. The author of *The Waffen SS: Hitler's Elite Guard at War, 1939-1945,* and editor and translator of *Hitler,* an anthology, he has also published numerous articles on modern European history. He served with the United States Air Force from 1953 to 1957.

Contents

Demolishing a Nation's Capacity for War

A worker dismantles a German coastal gun on the North Sea island of Helgoland in 1920 to comply with provisions of the Versailles treaty. Even as disarmament proceeded, however, German officers and industrialists were devising ways to evade the treaty and maintain Germany's military strength.

Stripped-down German warplanes, marked for export to Norway but impounded instead, await destruction near Berlin in 1919. In all, about 14,000 German planes were scrapped or seized by the victorious Allies.

Inspectors itemize the numbered fragments of milling machines at the Krupp Works in Essen. The great guns forged there brought Germany to the threshold of victory in World War I. After the war the Allies destroyed 60,000 tons of Krupp machinery, even as the firm's engineers secretly drew up plans for a new generation of weapons.

A mountain of condemned gun barrels lies ready for smelting at the Krupp Works in 1925. A year later the Allied supervisors of the disarmament program withdrew from Essen, allowing Krupp, in the words of its director, to prepare its new weapons for "mass production upon command."

Nr. 43. — 79. Jahrg.
Berlin, 24. Oktober 1926

Preis 60 Pfg.

Kladderadatsch

ONE

The Furtive Rebirth of Militarism

he June day was unseasonably warm, and the German soldiers and aviators marching in Berlin were unsuitably dressed for a three-hour parade. In combat they had worn tropical khaki outfits with Spanish insignia in a transparent attempt to conceal their identity, but such well-used uniforms would hardly be fitting for their triumphant return from the Spanish Civil War. So temporary uniforms had been tailored from bolts of thick brown wool. Now, as the heroes marched nine abreast down the broad Unter den Linden, they sweated, itched, and cursed under their breath. No discomfort, however, could dim the pride and patriotism that surged through the ranks as the line of march approached the reviewing stand. The troops broke into song: "Our enemies are the Reds, the Bolsheviks of the world."

As each rank passed the dais, the men snapped their heads smartly to the right on command to face two uniformed figures. One was their commander, Colonel Wolfram von Richthofen, a cousin of Manfred von Richthofen, the legendary Red Baron of World War I. Next to Richthofen stood another alumnus of the Great War, the former lance corporal Adolf Hitler.

On this sweltering June 6, 1939, the Führer and tens of thousands of Berliners had come to honor Nazi Germany's first veterans of combat, the famed Condor Legion. They were the pilots and technicians, gunners and tank-crew members—some 14,000 in all—who had helped win the Spanish Civil War for the Nationalist forces of Francisco Franco.

The occasion, however, marked an event far more significant than victory over the Spanish Republicans and their communist allies. The parade celebrated the rebirth of Germany's capacity to make war. Only two decades earlier, the German armed forces lay prostrate, defeated in combat and hobbled by the harsh terms of peace. Now, after three years' testing on the battlefields of Spain, the Reich's rebuilt military machine was proved ready. In less than three months, Hitler would turn it against neighboring Poland and thus ignite the Second World War.

Germany's phoenixlike rise from the ashes of World War I astounded the world. A testament to what the British historian John Wheeler-Bennett re-

Reflecting German hatred of the Versailles treaty, a 1926 Berlin magazine cover depicts the accord as a tombstone being toppled by hands rising from a grave labeled "Here lies the truth." Atop the stone are caricatures of France, Japan, Italy, Britain, and America.

ferred to as Germany's "phenomenal capacity for beating plowshares into swords," the revival owed much to the fanatical will and warped vision of the man on the reviewing stand. But Hitler's contribution was only part of the story, because German rearmament began long before he and his National Socialists rose to power in 1933.

The origins of the guns, tanks, and planes, even of the tactics and leadership that proved so effective in Spain, could be traced to the 1920s. They were products of a rearmament program instigated not by radical firebrands but by old-fashioned patriots, carried out largely in secret and financed by a series of liberal, democratically elected governments whose leaders chose to ignore that much of the program flouted the letter and spirit of Germany's treaty obligations.

The restorers of Germany's military strength had to overcome internal problems such as political instability and economic chaos. Yet the biggest obstacles facing them were the disarmament provisions of the Treaty of Versailles, which formally concluded World War I. Through the accord the victorious Allies sought to punish Germany and reduce it to a second-rate power. They imposed onerous reparations payments and other sanctions, took away Germany's colonies in Africa and the Pacific, and forced the Germans to cede sections of their homeland to France, Belgium, and Poland. But the most dramatic of the treaty's 440 articles and 75,000 words dealt with military disarmament.

The framers of the treaty sought to cripple Germany's fearsome military capacity forever. They destroyed or dismantled most of its weapons and the means of making new ones; they specifically deprived Germany of the four new weapons that had emerged during the war—airplanes, tanks, submarines, and poison gas—and systematically gutted the German armed forces. Under the treaty, for example, 14,000 military aircraft were turned over to the Allies or scrapped. The navy was reduced to a token force of fewer than 15,000 officers and men and an assortment of thirty-six prewar battleships, light cruisers, destroyers, and torpedo boats. In addition, most of the ships in the German merchant marine were confiscated as reparations payments.

But the proud old army, rich in the Prussian military tradition, sustained the fiercest blows under the treaty. Germany's prewar army had numbered two million. By the beginning of 1920—a timetable that was later extended by one year—the size of the army was slashed to a mere 100,000 officers and enlisted personnel. All had to be volunteers; conscription was banned. In order to prevent the creation of a trained reserve, the men were required to serve unusually long tours of duty (twenty-five years for officers, twelve years for other ranks). The vaunted German general staff was to be per-

The Versailles treaty altered the map of Germany, shown here as it was in 1922. Alsace-Lorraine, conquered by Germany in 1871, was restored to French rule; a sizable area in the east was returned to Poland; and part of the state of Schleswig was ceded to Denmark. Other areas formerly under German control were occupied temporarily by Allied troops or administered by the new League of Nations. Once Allied troops left the Rhineland, it was to remain demilitarized—that is, the Germans were forbidden to fortify the region or to station troops there.

OCCUPIED TERRITORY

LEAGUE OF NATIONS CONTROL

RHINELAND DEMILITARIZED ZONE

CEDED TERRITORIES

manently dissolved, and to forestall a rebirth of youthful martial spirit, military academies were closed. Tanks, heavy artillery, and poison gas were forbidden, and armored cars were allowed only for use by the police in riot control. Restrictions on allowable arsenals of small arms such as machine guns and rifles, and on the stockpiles of ammunition for them, were spelled out in meticulous detail.

Germany's compliance with the treaty was monitored by an Interallied Military Control Commission, which comprised inspection teams assigned to industry and to each branch of service—army and navy. The inspectors were uniformed personnel from five nations that helped frame the treaty: Great Britain, France, Italy, Belgium, and Japan. (An American delegation that was led by President Woodrow Wilson participated fully at Versailles, but the U.S. Senate refused to ratify the treaty, and no Americans were to serve on the inspection commission. "This isn't a treaty of peace," one member of the United States' delegation warned prophetically. "I can see at least eleven wars in it.")

The terms of the Versailles pact were announced on May 7, 1919, and their severity stunned the people of Germany. They felt outrage and betrayal. For one thing, most Germans rejected any sense of collective guilt for starting the war; they believed it had been forced upon them by the policies of France and Russia. Moreover, they had hoped that their radical change of governments during the waning days of the war—replacing the monarchy of Kaiser Wilhelm II with a parliamentary democracy—would soften the terms of peace. Pouring into the streets in protest, German citizens denounced what had emerged from Versailles as the "treaty of violence." Officers of the German navy were so furious that they scuttled the bulk of their fleet in order to prevent the Allies from confiscating it as conditions of the treaty dictated.

German president Friedrich Ebert, a socialist, labeled the treaty "unrealizable and unbearable"; however, his government had little choice but to accept it. An Allied naval blockade was starving the country, and if Germany resisted, it faced invasion by the French, British, and American armies still massed along the Rhine. Only nineteen minutes before the time limit set by the victors, the government yielded. Germany formally signed the detested treaty on June 28, 1919.

The government's concession contributed to an illusion zealously held by right-wing nationalists in and out of the army. As popular myth had it, the German army had not actually been defeated on the battlefield but had been stabbed in the back by the revolutionary government that deposed the monarchy and ratified the treaty. The reputation of any politician or government associated with the treaty was forever stained. This view of

events was so powerful that it resulted eventually in an armed putsch. In March 1920 elements of the army, led by a reactionary general, Walter von Lüttwitz, installed their own government in Berlin. At its head they placed an obscure civilian, a former agricultural official named Wolfgang Kapp, who had been born in New York. The other generals hesitated to move against their fellow soldiers, but a nationwide general strike led to the ouster of the upstarts in less than five days.

The desire to rearm grew stronger, and it infected more than just radical nationalists. Because the treaty left the armed forces scarcely able to maintain internal security and certainly incapable of defending Germany's borders in an unfriendly Europe, many German leaders were motivated by simple patriotism and the fear of foreign aggression. Others were driven by prospects for profit and renewed international influence. Whatever their motives, a diverse consensus of career officers, politicians, and industrialists rallied to the cause of *Wehrfreiheit*—military freedom. To achieve it, they were prepared to violate the terms of Versailles.

Major General Hans von Seeckt spoke for many when he wrote, "One thing no peace treaty, no foe, can take from us: manly thought. When fate again summons the German people to arms—and this day will inevitably come again—then it shall find a people of men, not weaklings, who will powerfully grip their trusted weapon. The form of this weapon is not so important, if hands of steel and hearts of iron employ it."

Less than a year after Seeckt wrote those ringing words, he was entrusted with the formidable task of shaping those "hands of steel and hearts of iron." In June of 1920, three months after the Kapp Putsch shook the military establishment, he was named *Chef der Heeresleitung*, or chief of army leadership, and placed in command of the new 100,000-man army. His command became widely known as the *Reichswehr*, for state defense, although the word technically applied both to the army and to the navy, which had its own commander.

At the age of fifty-four, Seeckt was in his prime, the model of a modern Prussian general. He carried his lean frame elegantly erect and wore a monocle in his left eye. In background as well as appearance, he embodied the classic German military tradition. The son of a general, he had entered the old imperial army in 1885 to serve in his father's elite unit, the Kaiser Alexander Guard Regiment. As a general-staff officer during World War I, he had distinguished himself on the eastern front by organizing the spectacular German breakthrough against the Russians at Gorlice in 1915, winning Prussia's highest military decoration, the Pour le mérite. (French was the court language of Prussia when the award was created in 1740.)

A Fleet Too Proud to Surrender

On November 21, 1918, ten days after the signing of the armistice that ended World War I, 370 British warships escorted the German High-Seas Fleet across the North Sea. Interned at the Scottish anchorage of Scapa Flow, the fleet rusted for seven months while the Versailles treaty was hammered out. By its terms, the German vessels—about seventy in all—were to be parceled out among the Allied navies.

To the ranking German officer at Scapa Flow, Vice Admiral Ludwig von Reuter, the thought of handing the fleet to former enemies was intolerable. There was no chance of making a run for it. But Reuter saw an opportunity to do the next best thing when the British sent most of his command back to Germany in June 1919, leaving aboard tiny crews that could quickly abandon ship. On June 17 Reuter dispatched secret letters to his captains, telling them to prepare to scuttle. Sailors made ready to open seacocks.

On June 21 Reuter gave the order: "Condition Z, scuttle!" Within minutes vessels began to founder—to the amazement of the British, who rushed about Scapa Flow in a frenzy, trying to save some of the captive ships. Twenty-three craft were kept afloat, including the destroyer G 102, seen flanked by tugs in the photograph at left. But the remaining two-thirds of the German fleet vanished beneath the waters.

Seeckt had the habit of maintaining long, mysterious silences, interspersed with occasional curt or caustic comments, a style that earned him the nickname of "Sphinx." But Seeckt, the precise and rigid Prussian, possessed more than what he called the "old spirit of silent, self-effacing devotion in the service of the army." Late in the war he had demonstrated patience, guile, and a flair for diplomacy in a series of difficult assignments aimed at reviving the flagging efforts of Germany's disheartened allies, Austria-Hungary and Turkey. He had also served as a member of the German delegation at Versailles. Having read and traveled widely, he could discuss music, art, or military tactics with equal facility, and in French or English as well as German. The British ambassador to Germany, Lord D'Abernon, observed that Seeckt had "a broader mind than is expected in so tight a uniform; a wider outlook than seems appropriate to so precise, so correct, so neat an exterior."

Thus equipped for his new command, Seeckt set out, as he wrote later, "to neutralize the poison" of the Versailles treaty. This meant not only overcoming the restrictions of the treaty itself but also smoothing the rifts and resentment caused by the government's ratification of it. The old officer corps, which the great German military theorist Carl von Clausewitz had characterized a century earlier as "a kind of guild, with its own laws, ordinances, and customs," had been responsible only to the kaiser. Now the kaiser had been replaced as head of state by a socialist who had begun his career as a saddle maker and tavern keeper. It was necessary that officers gain a new sense of loyalty, not necessarily to the republic or any other transient regime but to Seeckt's almost-mystical concept of the Reich, or nation, which he referred to as "the permanent substance of the German state and people."

At the same time, regular-army discipline had to be imposed upon the remnants of the *Freikorps*, or free companies, that remained in the Reichswehr. In the chaotic days immediately following the war, individual officers, acting on their own authority, had raised Freikorps volunteer units from the abundant ranks of veterans and eager, young, right-wing volunteers. These and other troops had formed the interim Provisional Reichswehr, approved by the government, that lasted until the Versailles treaty restructured the German army. Although the Freikorps had been vital to the preservation of public order and the protection of the eastern border during that period, they also had proved volatile and prone to joining rebellions such as the Kapp Putsch.

Seeckt insisted that the new Reichswehr remain aloof from politics. He banned membership in partisan organizations and blocked the circulation of blatantly political newspapers within the barracks. Even soldiers' con-

General Hans von Seeckt, chief of staff of the German Eleventh Army in World War I, confounded the Allies with his brilliant planning both during and after that war, when he rehabilitated the German army despite the strictures of Versailles.

stitutional right to vote in parliamentary elections was suspended during their tour of duty. Perhaps because Seeckt himself was a monarchist and made little attempt to conceal his distrust of parliamentary government, he was often accused of cracking down most severely on partisans of the left. But whatever his personal sympathies, he punished transgressors at both ends of the political spectrum. For example, he forcibly retired one general who was involved in rightist paramilitary groups and dismissed another, along with officers of lower rank, for supporting the embryonic Nazi party.

Virtually from the beginning, Seeckt found ways to circumvent the Versailles restrictions. He cleverly retained his vital general staff by hiding its functions under the innocuous heading of *Truppenamt,* or Troop Office, and by camouflaging its various branches with other bogus titles. The work of the staff's intelligence office, for example, proceeded in two phony agencies called the Statistical Section and the Welfare Office. He circumvented the abolition of military academies by creating a program of "special courses" within the army that accomplished the same goals.

To enlarge his corps of officers, which the treaty limited to 4,000, Seeckt secretly tucked his administrative personnel in jobs with civilian titles in the Defense Ministry and other government agencies, adding new staff to fill the imaginary vacancies. Seeckt also maintained an illegal force in order to defend the eastern frontiers of Germany against possible invasion by the newly reconstituted state of Poland. These troops, about 60,000 former Freikorps members and other irregulars inherited from the Provisional Reichswehr, were trained and supplied by the army and thinly disguised as civilian laborers. Known as the Black Reichswehr, they eventually had to be disbanded when their leaders involved them in antigovernment intrigue.

Seeckt also connived to build up the state police forces far beyond the Versailles limits and use them as a reservoir of military personnel. Combat-hardened officers put on police uniforms and gave military training to thousands of recruits. The Prussian police alone numbered 85,000, many of whom were equipped as infantry with rifles, machine guns, and even armored cars. Some of the specially trained German police would one day command army divisions and corps during World War II.

Seeckt decided that the Reichswehr's limited size was in some ways a virtue. It allowed him to be far more selective than he could have been with a large army of conscripts. For every vacancy among the rank and file, there was an average of seven applicants. Those chosen met the most demanding physical standards in the world. They received unusually high pay—about seven times that of their peers in the French army. And they were generally well treated by their officers, who were prohibited from inflicting the harsh and often brutal punishment that typified the old imperial army.

As in the old army, however, most of Seeckt's officers were drawn from aristocratic stock or from those upper- and middle-class families with strong military traditions. By 1925 fully half of the Reichswehr's generals were of noble birth. German officers, who were rigidly conservative by nature, made it difficult for Jews, socialists, communists, and other "undesirables"—including outspoken advocates of democracy—to enter the ranks as either officers or enlisted men.

But Seeckt made certain that merit was the main criterion for advancement after acceptance into the Reichswehr. For example, selection of officers to train with the new general staff, the so-called Troop Office, was based on competitive examinations. Those who completed three years of such training qualified to wear the coveted red trouser stripes signifying membership in the general staff. They became the elite of the Reichswehr and the nucleus of a future expanded army.

Seeckt made a virtue of necessity by developing a strategy of mobility to accommodate his diminutive, highly trained force. "The whole future of warfare," he wrote in 1921, "appears to me to be in the employment of mobile armies, relatively small but of high quality, and rendered distinctly more effective by the addition of aircraft." Although this emphasis on speed and maneuverability foreshadowed the German *Blitzkrieg*, or lightning war, it also reflected Seeckt's experiences on the relatively mobile eastern front during the First World War.

Seeckt's tactical views, in fact, were something of a contradiction. He was old-fashioned enough to question aloud whether tanks would ever replace horses, and he rebuked a subordinate who had the temerity to suggest that Reichswehr cavalry give up their lances. He refused to replace one unit's bicycles with motorcars. In any event, treaty limitations on his arsenal gave Seeckt no opportunity to test the tenets of motorized warfare on a realistic scale. Field training and maneuvers had to be staged with make-believe weapons such as plywood tanks and cannons with wooden barrels.

While stressing mobility, Seeckt structured the Reichswehr as a cadre for vast future expansion. He created what he called a *Führerheer*, or army of leaders, in which every member was trained to take on higher rank and responsibility at a moment's notice. Thus, in the event of mobilization, majors and colonels would become generals, and the most proficient of his

Wearing field glasses, General Seeckt *(center)* pays a visit in 1925 to students at the infantry school he founded at Dresden. Known for his civilized manner, Seeckt was nonetheless a combative man who once proclaimed that "war is the highest summit of human achievement."

noncommissioned officers could be promoted to lieutenants. Because the treaty did not limit the number of noncommissioned officers, an extraordinarily high complement of 40,000 sergeants and corporals—nearly one for every two privates—stood ready to step up in rank.

Seeckt's vision of an expanded army also was evident in his policy of keeping alive regimental traditions. Each infantry company, which typically numbered fewer than 300 men, was assigned the name, honors, and banners of a 3,000-troop regiment from the old imperial army. This not only enhanced morale but helped provide a practical blueprint for a tenfold expansion to a fighting force of a million soldiers.

The growing power and independence of the Reichswehr—and its commander—was demonstrated in 1923, when the infant Weimar Republic, named for the ancient town where its constitution was drafted, faced its

Carrying regimental banners from the old imperial army, troops of Seeckt's tradition-conscious Reichswehr goose-step in review past Paul von Hindenburg (*second from right*), German commander in chief during much of World War I.

most severe crisis. In January of that tumultuous year, the French army occupied the coal-rich Ruhr in a dispute over reparations payments. Inflation in Germany reached such heights that merely purchasing a single loaf of bread required a wheelbarrow laden with German marks. In September, when a right-wing separatist conspiracy threatened the large southern state of Bavaria and left-wing disturbances shook Thuringia and Saxony, President Ebert summoned Seeckt to an emergency meeting of the cabinet. "Will the army stick with us, General?" he asked anxiously. With evident pride and a touch of Prussian arrogance, Seeckt replied: "The army, Mr. President, will stick with me."

Soon thereafter, Ebert proclaimed a state of emergency that gave Seeckt near-dictatorial powers. For the next six months, the general virtually ran the government. His army put down uprisings of the extreme left and right, including the putsch started in a Munich beer hall by Adolf Hitler and his National Socialists.

While Seeckt was transforming the Reichswehr into the most powerful institution in Germany—he called it "a state within a state"—he was also strongly influencing foreign policy. This monarchist, who considered communism the nation's most serious internal threat, had an audacious plan: He wanted to enter an alliance with the bastion of Bolshevism, the Soviet Union. Both countries, he reasoned, shared an antipathy toward Poland. The Red Army, in fact, marched against the Polish capital during the summer of 1920, only to be turned back. Seeckt expressed his own feelings succinctly in a private memorandum: "Poland's existence is intolerable and incompatible with the survival of Germany."

The Soviet Union offered other major attractions for Seeckt. The Soviets were not a party to the Versailles treaty and thus had no stake in upholding it. And the vast reaches of Russia, so remote from the prying eyes of Allied observers, provided ideal sites for developing weaponry prohibited by the treaty and training the Reichswehr in its use. The Soviets, for their part, were likely to be receptive. They needed technical assistance and financial aid as they rearmed and rebuilt their own military, especially after the Poles repulsed the Red Army before Warsaw.

With the help of the German Foreign Office, Seeckt began secret negotiations with Russia early in 1920. He used several intermediaries, including Enver Paşa, a notorious Turkish adventurer and former minister of war. Paşa and Seeckt had become friends late in World War I when Seeckt was loaned to the Turkish army and served as chief of the Turkish general staff. When the Ottoman Empire collapsed in 1918, Seeckt helped Paşa get to Germany and thence to Moscow.

The negotiations between Germany and Russia led in 1922 to the Treaty of Rapallo, which reestablished commercial and diplomatic relations between the two unlikely partners. The agreement cast the first link in the

A Reichswehr supply column enters Dresden in November 1923 in support of troops suppressing a communist revolt. The soldiers were welcomed by townspeople; here, a young girl on a bicycle guides the troops.

chain that would lead to the Soviet-German nonaggression pact of 1939 and the partition of Poland.

Seeckt, meanwhile, organized a branch in his general staff known as *Sondergruppe R*—Special Group Russia—to do business with the Red Army. Their negotiations resulted in the establishment of two secret schools on Russian soil—an air base at Lipetsk and a tank center near Kazan—to train members of the Reichswehr. By 1925 German soldiers in civilian clothes had filtered clandestinely into the Soviet Union to learn to fly airplanes and drive tanks. The high-ranking Reichswehr officers who inspected the training centers traveled as members of a bogus communist workers' delegation from Germany, although almost all of them were nobles and monarchists.

Sondergruppe R also entered the world of commerce. Using government funds it formed a private trading concern known as GEFU, short for its innocent-sounding name, the Company for the Promotion of Industrial Enterprises. With technical help from German industry, GEFU founded and administered a string of factories in the Soviet Union dedicated to circumventing the Versailles treaty. One plant, in the province of Samara Bend, manufactured poison gas; another, at Fili near Moscow, built military aircraft and motors; and factories in Tula, Leningrad, and Schlüsselberg turned out artillery shells. The Reichswehr and the Red Army were to share the output of these plants, but only a shipment of 300,000 heavy artillery shells ever reached Germany.

Seeckt knew that the Soviet installations were merely a stopgap. Supplying enough arms and munitions for the expanded army he envisioned would depend upon "suitable arrangements" with industrialists at home in Germany. In 1924 Seeckt created the *Rüstungsamt*, a secret armaments office, in order to establish rapport with industrial leaders and to prepare detailed plans for mobilizing an army of sixty-three divisions. Seeckt was not interested in amassing stockpiles of arms that might soon become obsolete; instead, his aim was to encourage research and development. When the time came for full-scale rearmament, he wanted to have blue-

prints and prototypes for new, sophisticated weaponry that could be rushed into mass production.

The Reichswehr's entreaties found a mixed reception. While few industrialists had compunctions about violating the Versailles treaty by secretly cooperating with the army, many protested that they could not afford the financial sacrifices of clandestine research and development. But at least one titan of German industry fervently embraced Seeckt's schemes. He was Gustav Krupp von Bohlen und Halbach, head of the house of Krupp, world-renowned maker of steel and munitions. As early as January 1922 Krupp met privately with Seeckt and Admiral Paul Behncke, commander of the navy, and agreed—as Krupp wrote later—"to circumvent, and thereby break down, the provisions of the Treaty of Versailles that strangled Germany's military freedom."

German and Russian aviators and aircraft engineers *(right)* gather outside the Junkers factory at Fili, near Moscow. The plant turned out warplanes and trainers such as the Ju A-20 *(top right)*, equipped with skis for the snow-covered Soviet airstrips.

The two conspirators, Krupp and Seeckt, shared similarities and contrasts. Like Seeckt, Krupp was a monarchist who found the republic distasteful; indeed, he kept in touch with the deposed kaiser, Wilhelm II, writing him on his birthday every year. Krupp possessed, as did Seeckt, a shrewd and calculating mind. But in contrast to the elegant and suave general, Krupp was something of a comic-opera figure in appearance and manner. Small in stature—a head shorter than his wife—he had a domed forehead, set mouth, and gestures so quick and mechanical, an American writer noted, that they seemed to parody Prussian rigidity.

Krupp was obsessed with order and efficiency. Among a people who prided themselves on being on time, he became a legend for his punctuality. He lived each day by a precise and unvarying schedule and demanded the same of others. Each week he allotted his eight children exactly sixty minutes of his time for play, yet he took the time to read train schedules for typographical errors and, on finding one, to telephone the railroad and complain vociferously.

Despite the Krupp in his name, the curious little man had attained his eminence not by birth but through marriage. His wife, Bertha, was the granddaughter of Alfred Krupp, the eccentric "Cannon King" who began building guns for the Prussian army at Essen in 1861. The accuracy, range, and power of Alfred's artillery contributed greatly to the Prussian victory over France a decade later, and as a consequence, the Krupp dynasty prospered. Alfred built a 300-room castle, Villa Hügel, of glass, steel, and stone but not a stick of wood; even though his fortune depended upon the forges, fire terrified him. His son and heir Friedrich, who took over after Alfred's death in 1887, turned out to have more damaging eccentricities. In 1902 an account of Friedrich's homosexual behavior with young boys was published in Italian and German newspapers, and he killed himself.

The tragedy set the stage for the entrance of Gustav. Friedrich left the family business to his elder daughter Bertha. But in those days the notion of a woman presiding over a manufacturer of war matériel was unthinkable. Bertha needed a husband, and the matchmaker turned out to be none other than Kaiser Wilhelm II, who was such a close friend that the Krupps kept a suite in permanent readiness for him at Villa Hügel. From many available choices, the monarch tapped Gustav von Bohlen und Halbach, a minor diplomat and the offspring of Westphalian nobility with American connections. His mother was the daughter of a United States Army colonel who had fought in the American Civil War; his father, whose family had emigrated to Pennsylvania from Prussia, returned to Germany with money made from the family's holdings in the Scranton coalfields and received a title enabling him to use the honorific *von* in his name.

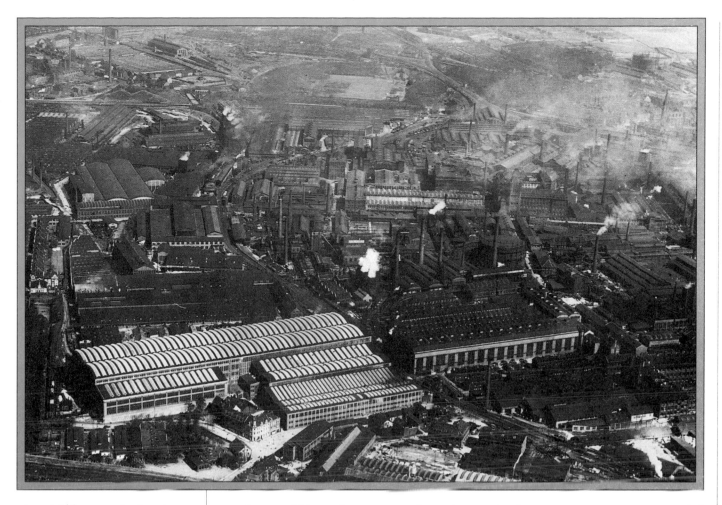

An aerial photograph taken in 1919 shows the vast Krupp factories at Essen in the heart of Germany's industrialized Ruhr. Within a month of the armistice, nearly half of the 105,000 workers at this arms-production center were laid off.

The wedding of Gustav and Bertha took place in 1906 under imperial auspices. Afterward, to perpetuate the dynasty in name, the kaiser conferred upon the bridegroom the right to add *Krupp* to his already-lengthy name and to pass it on, with the family fortune, to male heirs.

At the age of thirty-six, Gustav took charge of the company and set out, in the words of the kaiser's friendly challenge, to prove himself "a real Krupp." He modeled himself after Alfred, the old Cannon King, and the results were soon evident on the battlefronts of World War I. A peak wartime work force of 165,000 employees turned out such varied instruments of warfare as bayonets, battleship armor, artillery, shells, and a recent development, U-boats.

The Krupp firm produced as many as 3,000 field guns a month. The best-known of all its guns was Big Bertha, the huge seventeen-inch mobile howitzer named after Frau Krupp that could hurl a projectile weighing nearly a ton a distance of nine miles. An even more fearsome gun, Long Max, had a rifled barrel that was 112 feet long; during the spring and summer of 1918 it thundered and rained explosives on the city of Paris from a distance of seventy-five miles. For such accomplishments, Gustav was awarded the Iron Cross by the kaiser and the honorary degree of doctor of philosophy by Bonn University.

But Krupp and his company did not fare well under the Versailles treaty. He was cited, along with 900 other Germans, as a war criminal. Although the charges were later dropped, his firm was singled out for special attention. The treaty limited the concern to the manufacture of only enough

Barred by the Allies from producing war matériel, Krupp employees made trucks at Essen in a cavernous building 39,000 square meters in area. By 1923, when this photograph was taken, Krupp was testing American assembly-line methods.

cannon, armor, and other fittings to replace the components that had worn out on the navy's obsolescent battleships. It allowed Krupp to make one type of field gun at the rate of four per year. The bulk of the company's enormous munitions-manufacturing inventory, which had consisted at its wartime peak of nearly one million jigs, molds, presses, and other machines and had covered many acres in Essen and elsewhere, was dismantled or destroyed under the supervision of inspectors from the Interallied Military Control Commission. In addition, one-half of Krupp's steel-making capacity was taken away.

The process of disarmament at Krupp took a bizarre turn in one instance. An Allied inspector noted that the Germans had failed to surrender as many artillery pieces as were estimated in an inventory prepared by French intelligence; the Germans were about 1,500 guns short. A Krupp representative tried to explain that the French estimates were exaggerated. (Actually, the missing guns had been spirited across the border to a company in Holland owned by Krupp.) The impasse that developed over the guns was finally broken by the inspector. He ordered Krupp to resume full-scale production until there were enough artillery pieces to meet the French quota. The jigs and presses were then dismantled and the newly produced guns shipped off to be destroyed.

Krupp switched to peacetime production. His company had always turned out such nonmilitary items as railway wheels and machine tools, and now a new slogan appeared on the walls of its plants: *Wir machen alles!*—We make everything! Products ranging from baby carriages to lo-

comotives, from padlocks to cash registers, rolled off the lines. Krupp even manufactured a new kind of false teeth from stainless steel developed during the war. The metal had been used for the rust-resistant breech mechanisms in deck guns of submarines.

At the same time, however, Gustav Krupp began making preparations for massive rearmament. "If ever there should be a resurrection for Germany," he wrote later, "if ever she were to shake off the chains of Versailles, then Krupp would have to be prepared. The machines were demolished; the tools were destroyed; but one thing remained—the men, the men at the drawing boards and in the workshops, who in happy cooperation had brought the manufacture of guns to its last perfection. Their skill would have to be saved, their immense resources of knowledge and experience. I had to maintain Krupp as an armament factory for the distant future, in spite of all obstacles."

The ink was scarcely dry on the Versailles treaty when Krupp took advantage of one of its gaping loopholes. The disarmament provisions said nothing about German companies producing arms in other countries. Krupp looked first to Sweden and its Bofors steel and cannon works. He bought his way into Bofors by exchanging patents, licenses, and secret manufacturing processes for shares of stock. By late 1925 these holdings, plus additional shares purchased on the stock exchange with the help of covert subsidies from the German government, amounted to more than one-third of Bofors's stock—the controlling interest.

Well before he gained actual control, Krupp strongly influenced what came off the Bofors assembly lines. In 1921 he sent a chief engineer to oversee production, and soon the plant was assembling Krupp-designed artillery, antiaircraft guns, and even experimental ammunition for use against armored vehicles. Many of these products were sold in Holland, Denmark, and other countries. They turned a small profit for Krupp, enabled company designers to keep their hand in, and, not least, allowed Reichswehr officers who visited Bofors to learn the new technology. Eventually, visits by German officers aroused the suspicions of the Swedish government. In 1929 the carefully neutral Swedes outlawed foreign participation in the ownership of their munitions factories. Krupp's lawyers promptly circumvented the law by creating a holding company that camouflaged German involvement and kept Krupp in control of Bofors.

Krupp mounted an even more ambitious effort in Holland. In 1922, working covertly with the German admiralty, he set up in The Hague a concern known as IVS, which stood for Engineering Office for Shipbuilding. Its aim was to continue the now-forbidden submarine development begun at the Krupp shipyards in Kiel. Krupp moved his team of naval designers

to new yards in Holland, where IVS planned and made submarines for other nations. Through IVS Krupp also provided the technical expertise that helped foreign countries construct their own U-boats. He exchanged information with Japanese submarine builders and lent them his chief designer. He sent blueprints and naval architects to Finland, Spain, and Turkey, where they fabricated the precursors of the undersea fleets that would prowl the oceans during World War II. Those countries in turn permitted German commanders and crews to make trial runs in the new submarines, thereby providing experience the Germans could not acquire under their own flag.

Krupp secured his position in Holland by setting up holding companies and selling blocks of IVS stock to influential Dutch business people. It turned out to be a shrewd move. In 1926, when the French lodged an official protest about the flurry of submarine activity emanating from Holland, the Dutch government curtly made known that it would not interfere in matters of private business.

While Krupp evaded Versailles by developing weapons abroad, he took advantage of another loophole at home. Although the treaty ruled out the manufacture of new weapons in Germany, it did not prohibit their design on paper. Krupp maintained teams of weapons designers at Essen and fed them military and technical publications from all over the world to keep them abreast of the latest innovations. These teams generated a raft of inventions. A report filed by American army intelligence in May of 1921, less than one year after the signing of the treaty, indicated that Krupp recently had been awarded twenty-six patents for artillery-control devices, nine for fuses and shells, seventeen for field guns, and fourteen for heavy cannon that had to be transported by rail.

Krupp's home base was threatened with compromise early in 1923 by the French occupation of Essen and the rest of the Ruhr. Krupp hurriedly shipped all the company files and blueprints relating to rearmament to a hideout elsewhere in Germany. He also transferred his best team of artillery designers to Spandau, a district of Berlin, to continue their work.

In the Ruhr, German resentment of the French occupation grew daily, and although Krupp had counseled his workers to remain calm, a tragic confrontation occurred on company grounds on March 31, Easter Saturday. A detachment of French troops impetuously fired on a mass of Krupp workers, killing thirteen and wounding fifty-two. Afterward, a hastily convened French military court found Krupp guilty of instigating the incident and sent him to prison in Düsseldorf. After serving six months' time, he emerged from incarceration a national hero, with his resolve to rearm the Reich stronger than ever.

Thereafter, the pace quickened. In 1925 Krupp's artillery designers moved from Spandau to a building in the heart of Berlin in order to be closer to the liaison staff at Reichswehr headquarters. The team carefully maintained secrecy; even though the treaty did not ban design work, Krupp and his fellow rearmament planners feared a violent Allied reaction should their undertaking become public. In their offices on the tenth floor of 4 Potsdamer Platz, Krupp's designers operated in the guise of a fictitious machine-tool company named Koch and Kinzle. Neither the other tenants in the building nor members of the nearby Reichstag nor even the men's wives had any idea what they were up to. "Nobody noticed us, nobody bothered us, nobody even knocked on our door," recalled Fritz Tubbesing, one of the designers. "There we were, practically on top of the Reichstag, and they didn't know it."

Tubbesing and his colleagues churned out blueprints for cannon of all kinds. They developed plans for howitzers and light field guns, a new mobile mortar, and eight types of heavy artillery. Then they started on the design of another weapon forbidden by Versailles, the tank. For secrecy, they referred to it as an agricultural tractor.

Three submarines, designed by Krupp and built in Finland in the late 1920s, enter service with the Finnish navy. Before being commissioned, the vessels were tried out by crews from the German navy, which was forbidden its own U-boat fleet.

For all his stiffness, Krupp gloried in code names, covers, and the other trappings of secrecy. He loved duping "snoopers" from the Control Commission and the foreign press. He could even laugh at the rumors making the rounds. One story had it that the baby carriages Krupp produced could be taken apart and reassembled as machine guns. Another myth held that Krupp had preserved one of his Long Max cannons from the Great War by propping it upright and camouflaging it with brick so that the gun resembled a factory chimney.

The Krupp company financed its rearmament activities mainly through

French troops muster in Essen beside a statue of Alfred Krupp, founder of the arms-making dynasty.

Martyrs of a Bloody Saturday

On March 23, 1923—a day that would be known as Bloody Saturday—more than sixty workers at the Krupp plant in Essen were shot in a confrontation with French troops. The tragedy had its origins in the economic disaster that befell postwar Germany. With the mark's value plummeting and inflation running wild, Germany's leaders in late 1922 asked the Allied governments to temporarily suspend the heavy reparations payments mandated by the Treaty of Versailles. France's premier, Raymond Poincaré, refused, and when Germany later defaulted on a payment to France, Poincaré ordered French army units into the Ruhr region, the source of four-fifths of Germany's coal and steel.

Encouraged by the government in Berlin, the people of the Ruhr embarked on a campaign of passive resistance against the occupiers. In time, some workers resorted to acts of sabotage. The frustrated French retaliated by placing the ringleaders under arrest and condemning some of them to death.

The inevitable explosion took place on Easter Saturday, when a detachment of French soldiers entered a Krupp warehouse to take inventory of the vehicles there. Factory sirens blared and workers streamed in from every corner of the plant to confront the troops. The head of the firm, Gustav Krupp, was in his office nearby but made no attempt to disperse the angry crowd. Surrounded, the French troops set up a machine gun at the entrance to the building they had occupied. Then a few Krupp workers made their way to the roof and toyed with the heating valves so that the building filled with steam.

Unnerved, the soldiers fired into the crowd, killing thirteen workers and wounding fifty or more.

The dead were hailed as martyrs in Germany and received an elaborate funeral. Krupp was arrested and tried by the French on the charge that he had incited the incident by sounding the company sirens. A court sentenced him to fifteen years in prison.

Krupp's internment turned out to be brief and relatively benign. His German jailers kept the door to his cell unlocked and allowed visits from family members and associates. Important international figures, including the pope, called for his release, and in December of 1923, after serving scarcely six months, he was granted a Christmas amnesty by the French, who soon withdrew the last of their harried troops from the Ruhr.

Gustav Krupp, shown shortly after his marriage into the Krupp family in 1906, was likened by his French prosecutor to a German general who smiled as his "troops burned French villages."

Escorted by Krupp miners in their ceremonial guild costumes, the coffins of workers killed by French troops ride on a flower-bedecked hearse during the lavish funeral in April 1923.

the production of baby carriages, locomotives, and other nonmilitary items. There were, however, less conventional sources of funds. The parliamentary government that Krupp so disliked provided subsidies estimated as high as $300 million. And thanks largely to the work of Otto Wiedfeldt, a Krupp board member who served four years as German ambassador in Washington, in 1925 the United States furnished two loans totaling $10 million to help the company survive a period of ruinous inflation.

Krupp also hoped to gain funding from Britain under an old patent agreement with Vickers' Sons and Maxim, the arms manufacturer. Around the turn of the century, the Krupp firm had leased the use of a patent to Vickers for a special fuse that detonated artillery shells. In return Vickers was supposed to pay a little more than a shilling for each fuse manufactured. After the war Krupp demanded payment of £260,000 from Vickers, an amount based on estimates of German artillery casualties sustained on the British fronts. Krupp ultimately settled for a fraction of that, £40,000. Even so, he was profiting directly from German casualties in one war while helping prepare for another.

At the same time Krupp worked to equip future German armed forces with the latest in weaponry on land or sea, other Germans labored to keep alive

the potential for another vital weapon forbidden by Versailles, the airplane. Despite the ban, German aviation in the 1920s enjoyed a revival that was so vigorous it laid the foundation for the vaunted Luftwaffe, providing much of its leadership and the forerunners of its fighting planes.

It was the sport of gliding, in fact, that spurred the spontaneous revival of aviation. As one chronicler of the period wrote, "By the beginning of 1922, almost the only things German that could be seen flying in German skies were birds and homemade gliders." Lured by their love

Spectators crowd the Wasserkuppe, a knob in the Rhön Mountains, as a glider soars during a flying-club meet in 1924. Young Germans' yen to fly—if only in crude gliders such as the one being tested at left—found a practical outlet in 1926, when restrictions on the production of powered civil aircraft in Germany were ended.

of flying, university students and World War I pilots constructed gliders from whatever scraps of wood, wire, and cloth they could scrounge. They designed their craft so they could be broken down into sections and packed in crates for transport, especially by rail to the Rhön Mountains in central Germany, where annual competitions were held.

Many of the competing pilots had no money. They slept in the packing crates and hauled their craft on towropes to the summit of the Wasserkuppe, there to be launched into the thermal updrafts for a glorious few minutes of free flight. "We young Germans who traveled to the Rhön, starving and freezing, did so without any idea of a war of revenge in the future," wrote Hermann Steiner, a bomber pilot during World War I. "We did it because we did not want to give up our dream of flying."

In addition to nurturing the spirit and skill of flying, gliding stimulated aeronautical research. The Rhön contests attracted many of the best minds in German aviation. Aircraft manufacturer Anthony Fokker, future fighter-plane designer Willy Messerschmitt, theorist Theodor von Kármán—all soared in the fierce competitions there and learned from the performances of their fragile craft. Their gliders, for example, quickly demonstrated the aerodynamic advantages of a single long-span wing over the double- and triple-wing arrangements of powered flight popular during World War I. The sleek, single-wing warplanes that later took to German skies owed much to the slender, gull-like gliders that evolved during the 1920s.

The omnivorous general Seeckt kept a close eye on gliding and its enthusiastic pilot-designers. He attended the Rhön competition one year, accompanied by his air technical officer, Captain Kurt Student, and ar-

ranged for Reichswehr funds to be funneled through the Ministry of Transport to subsidize experiments in powerless flight.

Seeckt, despite his interest in such anachronisms as the horse cavalry, was forward-looking enough to envision an independent air arm. He created special aviation sections in his disguised general staff and made room in his tight officer corps for 180 veteran pilots from World War I. He distributed these "special-duty consultants" throughout his major commands in an attempt to instill air-mindedness. It was their mission, for example, to make certain that infantry commanders on maneuvers take into account the possible actions of planes, friend and foe, when planning their tactics.

In 1924 the Reichswehr took advantage of newly relaxed Allied restrictions on powered flight by covertly funding a new aviation club called Sportflug, or Sport Flying. It set up throughout Germany ten schools ostensibly intended to train private pilots. In fact, the schools provided

A Ju 26 passenger plane bears the name *Lufthansa*, the German state airline founded in 1926. As its appearance suggests, the three-engine transport was slow yet reliable. A descendant, the Ju 52, became the workhorse cargo and troop carrier of the German air force in the 1930s.

The so-called *Sportflug*, or sport flying, clubs formed in Germany in the mid-1920s had a military flavor. At left, members of a group perform army-style calisthenics in shirts stamped with the club's emblem; the same insignia adorned the club's training planes, such as the Heinkel HD 21 at top left.

refresher courses for veteran army fliers and trained new pilots for the Reichswehr. Seeckt was even able to arrange for an aviation reserve using pilots and ground crews of Lufthansa, the new government airline.

Advanced training in actual fighter planes became available in 1925 with the opening of a secret air base Seeckt had negotiated in the Soviet Union. Situated at Lipetsk, about 220 miles southeast of Moscow, the base was staffed by both Germans and Russians but disguised as a purely Soviet air-force installation. Security was so elaborate that trainees traveled there under assumed names and received their mail through a Berlin box number. Three fliers killed at the base in accidents were shipped home in wooden crates labeled "spare parts."

About 220 German pilots and other flight personnel—including three future field marshals of the Luftwaffe—completed six-month training courses that were conducted over the next eight years. An additional 750 ground-crew and administrative personnel also were trained at Lipetsk. Many of the Germans even took part in maneuvers with the Red Army, developing with Russian assistance the tactics of close air-ground support that the Luftwaffe would later apply with such devastating effect.

The development of German aircraft proceeded in a similar clandestine manner. Provisions of the Versailles treaty and subsequent Paris Air Agreements combined to prohibit the manufacture of military aircraft in Germany and limit that of civilian airplanes. Owing to Allied stalling tactics, the Germans were prevented from producing planes of any kind for two years

following the war. After that, the Allies allowed the building of some civilian craft but imposed strict limits on their performance characteristics. No plane could fly faster than 105 miles per hour or higher than 13,000 feet, carry more than 1,300 pounds of payload, or exceed 186 miles in range.

All of these restrictions were pegged at levels well below the technical standards of the day. They continued in effect until 1926. Then German civil air authorities invoked a fine point in the treaty requiring that all non-German planes operating within the Reich conform to the same limitations applied to German aircraft. When the Germans began impounding French and British airliners, the Allies lifted the restrictions.

In the meantime, many of Germany's airframe and engine manufacturers went out of business. Several who survived did so by setting up shop abroad. Adolf Rohrbach opened a plant in Denmark, where he built large flying boats and developed the smooth metal skin with flush rivets that eventually became common on aircraft everywhere. Hugo Junkers located a factory in Sweden. At the behest of the Sondergruppe R, Junkers in 1924 also constructed and began to operate the Soviet aircraft plant at Fili that made reconnaissance planes for the Red Air Force.

Anthony Fokker, the irrepressible young Dutchman who had made a fortune manufacturing some of Germany's best World War I fighter planes, moved his business to Holland in 1920, duping Allied inspectors. When the commission members visited his plant at Schwerin in northern Germany, they found enough planes and parts to think that all of Fokker's assets were accounted for. But Fokker's export manager had removed more than half of the inventory, including 220 planes, 400 engines, and many spare parts, hiding it in barns, cellars, and stables in the surrounding countryside. Then, with the connivance of the German government, he smuggled everything into Holland by rail, a feat that required 350 carloads.

Fokker renounced his German citizenship and reopened for business in Amsterdam. But he retained his ties with Germany, a move that paid off during the Ruhr crisis of 1923. Seeckt persuaded the government to secretly order 100 Fokker fighter planes and smuggle them into Germany for possible use in defending the Reich against the French. At that moment, they were the fastest military planes in the world, with a top speed of 171 miles per hour. The crisis ended before the aircraft were ready for delivery, so Fokker sold the first 50 fighters to Rumania. Germany quietly purchased the other 50 and shipped them to the secret Reichswehr base in the Soviet Union for use in training German pilots.

One fledgling manufacturer, Ernst Heinkel, kept his operations in Germany and engaged in what he called "a daring game of hide-and-seek" with inspectors from the Control Commission. A successful aircraft designer

A Fokker D XIII fighter speeds above the airfield at Lipetsk in the late 1920s. The German biplane, reminiscent of Fokker's brilliant World War I designs, was rendered obsolete by the monoplanes of the 1000s but was still used as a trainer.

during the war, Heinkel founded a small company in 1921 and flagrantly violated the treaty in collaboration with the American and Japanese navies, who contracted him to build a small floatplane that could be carried on a submarine. Heinkel later designed and constructed a seaplane for the Swedes. The components were made at his factory in the town of Warnemünde on the Baltic Sea and assembled in Sweden.

Heinkel's business soon expanded, and so did the risks. In 1923 the Reichswehr secretly commissioned a speedy reconnaissance biplane capable of mounting a single machine gun. The Japanese wanted a similar plane, plus an aircraft to be armed with torpedoes. Heinkel relished all the business but fretted about how he could hide so many different military prototypes from the Allied inspectors. His Japanese customers helped solve the problem. Japan's naval attaché in Berlin was a member of the Control Commission and hence privy to the inspectors' plans. Every time they scheduled a visit to Heinkel's plant, an accomplice of the diplomat telephoned Heinkel from Berlin with a coded warning. Thus alerted, his workers immediately loaded all the airplane parts into waiting trucks and hid the incriminating evidence a few miles away among the sand dunes until the inspectors had gone. The only intruder who was able to catch Heinkel red-handed was the Reichswehr's own air technical officer, Captain Student, who climbed the high wire fences around the factory to demonstrate lapses in security.

The Interallied Military Control Commission could not begin to uncover all the deceptions by which the Germans evaded the disarmament pro-

visions of the Versailles treaty. The commission lacked the personnel to keep the army and the navy, giant industries such as Krupp's, and small plants such as Heinkel's under constant scrutiny. To make matters worse for the Allies, the Reichswehr's counterintelligence branch, known as the *Abwehr*, tuned in to the commission's plans. By tapping telephone lines and intercepting radio transmissions, the Abwehr provided timely warnings of inspections to both the military and private industry. And few Germans were willing to serve as informants for the commission. Most were deterred by the prospect of retaliation: Vigilantes sometimes committed murder to silence informants.

Even so, the commission and the Allied governments were not nearly as gullible as Gustav Krupp and other Germans believed. Commission inspections, gleanings of their national intelligence services, and occasional reports from informants all pointed to a German effort to rearm. There were even highly revealing newspaper reports, including an exposé of the Reichswehr's collaboration with the Red Army, published in 1926 by England's *Manchester Guardian.*

What was lacking was not information but the will to do anything about it. A combination of circumstances caused the Allied powers to largely ignore Germany's military renaissance. They were preoccupied with problems at home and loath to enforce the treaty by going to war again. They knew that the Reichswehr was no match for the French army, with its 612,000 troops and a trained reserve of six times that many. Even Poland, which had 266,000 men in uniform and an air force of 1,000 planes, was more powerful than Germany.

Perhaps most important, the members of the Control Commission believed assurances from the German government that it would preserve the peace. In 1925 Germany signed the Locarno Pact along with France, Great Britain, Italy, and Belgium; the signatories agreed not to wage war against one another for a period of at least thirty years. Germany's admission into the League of Nations only nine months later was the final signal of the nation's reacceptance by the framers of the Treaty of Versailles. The able German foreign minister, Gustav Stresemann, had conducted such a vigorous campaign to assure the world of the Reich's noble intentions—while secretly supporting his country's illicit rearmament—that he shared the Nobel Peace Prize in 1926.

Convinced of Germany's peaceable posture, the Allies withdrew the Control Commission from Germany early in 1927, five years ahead of schedule. The British, French, and Belgian governments were so eager to extract the commission that they ignored its final report, which presented a withering account of its most recent inspection of the Reichswehr and

German industry. According to a British general who had served on the commission, the 500-plus pages in the report could be boiled down to one damning indictment: "Germany had never disarmed, had never had the intention of disarming, and for seven years had done everything in her power to deceive and 'counter-control' the commission appointed to control her disarmament."

Ironically, just as the shackles of Versailles were shaking loose, a series of events threatened to disrupt the German rearmament program. Since the end of the war, the conservative German military establishment had collaborated closely with a parade of liberal governments—a dozen different cabinets in only six years—despite sharp ideological differences. For the most part, cabinet members either approved of rearmament or refused to oppose it. Then, in the autumn of 1926, Seeckt touched off a crisis. The old monarchist permitted Prince Wilhelm, grandson of the deposed kaiser,

An He 12 floatplane is catapulted from the German ocean liner *Bremen.* Designed in 1929, the He 12 was used to speed delivery of international mail. Launched while the vessel was far from port, the plane raced ahead with the post, reducing delivery time.

to take part in Reichswehr maneuvers as a uniformed officer. Although the appearance of the prince was meant to be ceremonial, it struck a raw nerve in the republican government.

Currents of nationalism still ran deep in Germany, and the prince's presence symbolized for many the restoration of the old Germany—the ideal state, ruled by monarch and military. The liberal government had reason to fear anything that might kindle the smoldering emotions of the ultraconservatives and lead to another coup attempt. Moreover, the incident clearly violated the Versailles treaty's requirement that Reichswehr officers had to serve twenty-five-year tours of duty, and it came at a time when delicate negotiations were under way for withdrawal of the Control Commission. Seeckt had acted, as he often did, without consulting even his nominal superior, Defense Minister Otto Gessler. To many in the government, it was one more example—and one too many—of Seeckt's arrogance and contempt for parliamentary democracy. In the resulting furor, Seeckt was forced to resign after serving for nearly seven years as the chief architect of German rearmament.

Then came two more controversies that were damaging to the Reichswehr. In December 1926, two months after Seeckt's departure, former Chancellor Philipp Scheidemann publicly attacked on the floor of the Reichstag the army's illicit involvement with training and munitions production in the Soviet Union. Scheidemann, whose face was scarred from acid hurled years earlier by a would-be assassin, provoked bitter criticism from both the communist left and the nationalist right; he received hundreds of death threats. But his revelations brought down the cabinet and forced the Reichswehr to curtail its Soviet operations. A year later, Defense Minister Gessler resigned after revelations that his subordinates, trying to raise money for rearmament, had covertly invested ministry funds in risky private ventures, including a motion-picture production company that went bankrupt. But these setbacks to rearmament proved to be only temporary. The parliamentary concern about controlling the military soon lapsed, and the power of the Reichswehr continued to increase. One measure of its autonomy was its budget, which doubled in the four years between 1924 and 1928.

With government largesse paving the way and the nearsighted Allied inspectors no longer snooping about, the arms industry stepped up its efforts. Emphasis shifted from the design of weapons to the production of prototypes. Although the Versailles treaty was still in effect, upstart aircraft makers and designers such as Heinkel and Messerschmitt began turning out warplanes more openly. Krupp summoned home a group of his naval engineers who had been building submarines in Holland and resettled

Berliners in frayed suits eat a meal outside a soup kitchen during the Great Depression. The economic collapse hit virtually every segment of German society, creating vast discontent that Hitler would exploit in his rise to power.

them in Kiel. There they worked on the first of three vessels that would be known as pocket battleships because of their relatively small size and powerful armaments. These ships were authorized under the treaty to have a maximum displacement of 10,000 tons, but Krupp and the navy blithely made them 17 percent heavier.

Krupp's team of ordnance designers in Berlin also saw their paperwork become real. In 1928 their blueprints for "agricultural tractors" were transformed into the first tanks produced in Germany since the war. Krupp realized that the earlier destruction of much of his munitions-making equipment was a blessing, because it eliminated what would have grown obsolete. He now had up-to-date technology and was preparing for "mass production upon command."

The command would have to wait. In 1929 the worldwide depression took Germany in its grasp, and economic forces—succeeding where the politicians had failed—slowed the momentum of rearmament. With millions of German citizens out of work and many banks out of money, the process of rebuilding the nation's military took a backseat to more urgent problems. But these same economic forces soon would be responsible for greatly accelerating the arms buildup. They brought to center stage Adolf Hitler and his hypnotic vision of a militant German Reich not merely restored, but invincible. ✚

Every Man a Leader

"Defenseless is honorless" was the guiding maxim of General Hans von Seeckt, the brilliant military administrator who oversaw the creation of Germany's new army, the Reichswehr. Undaunted by the restrictions levied on Germany's armed forces by the Treaty of Versailles, Seeckt started an ambitious program of "mental and spiritual rearmament" that emphasized soldierly skills and initiative rather than technological might. "Material is superior to the living, mortal human mass," Seeckt wrote, "but it is not superior to the living and immortal human mind."

With conscription abolished and German forces limited to 100,000 troops, the Reichswehr could be extremely selective in its choice of recruits. Volunteers were required to pass a battery of physical and mental tests; enlisted men had to sign on for a minimum of twelve years, officers for twenty-five. Once in the ranks, each soldier was trained as a specialist, with emphasis placed on leadership abilities. Since formal military academies had been abolished by the Versailles treaty, Seeckt initiated a system of military education at the company and regimental levels. Privates received training as noncommissioned officers, and the NCOs were trained as officers; in the event of war, the army could rapidly be increased in size, with every man qualified to move up at least one grade in rank.

The newfound pride and proficiency of the Reichswehr were tested in large-scale war games held during semiannual maneuvers. Denied the use of tanks, antiaircraft guns, and other modern military hardware, the Germans made do with cleverly constructed mockups of cardboard and wood. So-called enemy aircraft were occasionally represented by toy balloons, while an individual soldier might display a placard that proclaimed, "I am a platoon" or "This is a machine-gun nest of eight men." The Reichswehr, however, was no laughing matter. "That army," conceded one foreign observer, "has engaged the attention of every general staff in the world."

Mounted troops advance at a gallop during maneuvers in 1930.

Civilian spectators watch as Reichswehr cavalry cross the Elbe River as part of the 1930 maneuvers. In wartime, the horsemen were supposed to scout ahead of the main army and pursue a defeated enemy.

The old-fashioned cavalry, mandated by Versailles, provided surprisingly good training for future tank officers.

A machine-gun squad uses semaphore to communicate with another unit. In 1930 such visual signals had become obsolete.

Inside a truck used as headquarters, a staff officer (*right*) and a sergeant trace troop movements during exercises.

Radio personnel stand by their station in a mock gas attack. German radios were among the world's most advanced.

A machine-gun detachment covers an artillery unit's flank as an observer uses a range finder to direct fire on enemy positions.

Dummy tanks of cardboard and tin mounted atop automobiles simulate an armored attack. Since the Versailles treaty also

banned antitank guns, the Reichswehr drilled with full-scale wooden replicas *(inset)*.

TWO

A Corporal Courting the Generals

T

he case became a cause célèbre long before it reached the courtroom. Early in 1930 three young army lieutenants stationed at Ulm in southern Germany were charged with spreading National Socialist propaganda among their fellow Reichswehr officers. Such activity violated the strict rules against political partisanship imposed a decade before by General Hans von Seeckt. But the defendants had done worse: They had tried to persuade their comrades that the government was not worth defending, and that they should stand by without firing a shot if the Nazis staged an armed revolt. This offense amounted to high treason.

Reichswehr officials attempted at first to keep the case quiet. They were aware of unhappiness among many young officers. Much of the discontent stemmed from a provision in the Versailles treaty that limited the size of the army to 100,000 men—and thereby severely restricted the chance of promotion through the ranks. Increasingly, the young officers turned an ear to the Nazis, who promised to eliminate the obstacle to advancement by greatly expanding the Reichswehr. Fearing that publicity from the Ulm case would only enhance the appeal of the Nazis and fuel the unrest in the officer ranks, army leaders hoped to treat the matter as a routine breach of discipline and resolve it before an army court-martial. But one of the defendants forced the army's hand. He wrote an inflammatory account of the case and had it smuggled from his jail cell to a Nazi newspaper. Once his article had been published, the resulting wave of publicity compelled the army to pass the case to a civilian court.

The ensuing drama was heightened even more by the results of the recent Reichstag elections. On September 14, 1930, only nine days before the trial began in the Supreme Court in Leipzig, the Nazis achieved their first major breakthrough at the polls. Their candidates received more than six million votes; they had garnered a mere 810,000 two years earlier. And by winning 107 of the Reichstag's 577 seats—versus 12 in 1928—the Nazis became second only to the Social Democrats in the parliament.

Testimony at the trial indicated that pro-Nazi sentiment was widespread in the army as well. Defense witnesses, including Colonel Ludwig Beck,

Presidential aspirant Adolf Hitler strides from a chartered aircraft during the 1932 campaign. In a two-week tour, he crisscrossed the nation, visiting forty-six cities and speaking to tens of thousands of new supporters.

who commanded the defendants' artillery regiment and in four years would be named chief of the general staff, spoke of the low morale and disaffection among the young officers. More disturbing to the government, Beck and other witnesses revealed their sympathy with the defendants.

But the dramatic high point of the trial came when a civilian took the stand. This star witness for the defense was the Nazi party's charismatic leader, Adolf Hitler. His appearance had little to do with the actual defense of the accused. In fact, he wanted to downplay the evidence of Nazi sentiment in the army and dispel any other notions that might alienate the leaders of the Reichswehr. His primary purpose in appearing in the Leipzig courtroom was to woo the generals.

Hitler's performance was a tour de force. He spoke for hours, mustering all his oratorical skills and subtle mastery of political strategy. He indignantly denied that his Nazis intended to seize power through armed revolt; the party would rely on constitutional means only. He lashed out at the Versailles treaty, which bound Germany "hand and foot," and vowed to fight it "by every means, even though the world looks on these means as illegal." He scoffed at the notion that his growing army of brown-shirted Storm Troopers, the Sturmabteilung (SA), was intended for anything more than "the purpose of protecting the party in its propaganda."

Above all, Hitler continued, neither the Storm Troopers nor any other party organization constituted a threat to the military supremacy of the Reichswehr. "I have always held the view that any attempt to replace the army was madness," he declared. "None of us has any interest in replacing the army. We will see to it, when we have come to power, that out of the present Reichswehr a great army of the German people shall arise."

Only toward the end of his testimony did Hitler stop courting the generals long enough to play to his partisans, who packed the gallery. When the party comes to power, he said, "there will be a National Socialist Court of Justice" and "heads will roll." At this, his supporters cheered and applauded wildly. Afterward they carried him in triumph from the Palace of Justice to the train station, where a special Pullman car waited to return him to the city of Munich.

In all the excitement, the outcome of the trial seemed an afterthought. The three defendants were found guilty of conspiracy to commit high treason. But their mild sentences—eighteen months of easy confinement for each—reflected the growing indifference and even hostility toward the Weimar Republic, a national malaise that the Nazis intended to exploit.

Hitler's virtuoso performance in Leipzig was part of his campaign to win over the nation's power elite. In addition to soliciting the votes of the masses, he wanted to forge an alliance with the leaders of the Reichswehr and the titans of industry. It was not a task that Hitler relished, for at heart he was a petit bourgeois who distrusted generals and capitalists. But he realized that the Nazis could not take control of Germany without the favor, or at least the sufferance, of the army and its industrial allies. Once he held the reins of power, he intended to use the alliance with the military and big business to realize his vision of a new German empire.

In his courtship of the Reichswehr, Hitler exerted a broad appeal. He offered an attractive alternative in a depression-crippled economy that now had almost six million unemployed, and a chaotic political system in which as many as ten parties vied for control of the Reichstag. He struck a chord in the hearts of soldiers with his vehement denunciations of the Versailles treaty, his promise of a greatly expanded army, and his call for the restoration of Germany's lost glory and prestige.

Hitler's military credentials endeared him especially to the young officers and the rank and file. He had been one of them, a corporal who served with distinction during the Great War. As a dispatch runner on the western front, he had been awarded the Iron Cross, First Class—a rare honor for a soldier of low rank. He professed to revere the military and described his tour of duty as the happiest period of his life. He liked to refer to himself as "the unknown soldier of the world war."

Hitler was also making headway with senior officers, who eagerly anticipated full-scale rearmament. For many such men, the eventful September of 1930, with its Nazi gains at the polls and Hitler's testimony at Leipzig, marked a turning point. According to Alfred Jodl, a promising officer who would figure in the German command structure during World War II, Hitler had succeeded in reassuring many skeptical colonels and generals that he had no intention of undermining the army. Even Seeckt, the retired army commander who had just been elected to the Reichstag, showed signs of endorsing the Nazis. But the leadership of the Reichswehr remained steadfastly opposed to Hitler and the Nazis. "The Reichswehr will never allow them to come to power," the army commander, General Kurt von Hammerstein, assured a civilian friend.

Equally adamant resisters of nazism were the three key figures in the German government. Each man in this triumvirate was a nationalist, a conservative, and a distinguished veteran of the Great War. Paul von Hin-

The message "Our last hope: Hitler" is superimposed over downtrodden Germans in this campaign poster. Between the Reichstag elections of 1930 and 1932, Nazi propaganda exploited the erosion of public confidence in the Weimar Republic.

denburg, the president since 1925 and now an octogenarian, had commanded the German army during the war and was the nation's most renowned soldier. The chancellor was Heinrich Brüning, the scholarly leader of the Catholic Center party who had led his machine-gun company with such gallantry that he, too, had been been awarded the Iron Cross, First Class—an award held by five other members of his cabinet. The defense minister, Wilhelm Groener, had been first quartermaster general at the end of the war, as well as Hindenburg's deputy.

Groener was the government's most vigorous opponent of Hitler—and one of Germany's ablest public servants. He had been that rarity among the leaders of the old imperial army: a general who was neither Prussian nor noble in origin. Born in 1867 in southwestern Germany, the son of a noncommissioned officer, he performed several vital staff jobs during the early years of World War I, including the organization of the railroads. During the last days of the war he helped to pave the way for an armistice by persuading the kaiser to go into exile and abdicate his crown because he no longer commanded the loyalty of the army. Groener then aided the country's transition to a postwar republic by organizing the orderly return and demobilization of the army.

These accomplishments, together with subsequent service as minister of transportation from 1920 to 1923, had won Groener a reputation as the "democratic general." In fact, like Seeckt and other generals, he had been a traditionalist who favored the restoration of the monarchy. But as defense minister since 1928, he had cooperated closely with a series of parliamentary governments because he was a patriot in the truest sense.

Groener launched his first counterattack against Hitler nearly a year before the Leipzig trial. In November of 1929 he issued a sharp decree to the Reichswehr, warning that the Nazi party "aims at the disintegration" of the army. Two months later, in a general order, he likened the Nazis to the communists and charged that "in order to use the army for the political aims of their party, they attempt to dazzle us." The Reichswehr, he concluded, has only one goal: "To serve the state, far from all party politics, to save and maintain it against the terrible pressure from without and the insane strife at home."

In the months that followed the trial, Groener's concern focused increasingly on Hitler's growing legion, the SA. The Storm Troopers looked and acted more like an army all the time—albeit a tyrannical one. They wore uniforms, marched in formation with bands and banners, and occasionally broke ranks in order to beat up opponents and disrupt the political rallies of their rivals.

Hitler's disclaimers about the Storm Troopers were sincere. He never

Minister of Defense Wilhelm Groener *(left)* and President Paul von Hindenburg observe Reichswehr maneuvers. Groener in 1932 persuaded Hindenburg to prohibit the Nazis' paramilitary SA and SS, insisting that only the state had the right to maintain such forces.

intended for them to challenge the role of the army and had long opposed the military ambitions of his Nazi comrade Ernst Röhm, leader of the SA. That issue had precipitated a break between the two men in 1925 and led to Röhm's resignation and self-imposed exile in Bolivia. But in January 1931, three months after the Leipzig trial, Hitler brought Röhm back from South America and placed him in command of the SA once again. Röhm strengthened his army of Storm Troopers, which already numbered about 250,000 men. He instituted a program of rigorous military training and swept up new recruits from the ranks of the disaffected by offering them a uniform, comradeship, and a cause.

Groener considered the revitalized SA a threat to the army and a menace to the state. He decided to put the Storm Troopers out of business by

A column of trucks packed with SA Brownshirts chanting "Germany, awake!" rumbles through Munich during the 1932 election campaign. The staged event was part of propagandist Joseph Goebbels's "war of posters and banners."

Chiemgau Sturm 10 Trupp Traunstein

banning them. But he had to move cautiously because of strong dissent within the Reichswehr. Some of this opposition arose from resentment of Groener himself. Many old-line officers never forgave him the role he played in exiling the kaiser. Others distrusted his policy of cordial cooperation with the republic and criticized his failure to prevent the Leipzig trial. Moreover, many officers wanted to preserve the SA as an auxiliary force in case of war with Poland or as a brown-shirted repository for the nation's unemployed youth.

To disarm his critics, the embattled defense minister planned to create a 200,000-man militia made up of conscripts. Groener saw the idea as a bold way to seize the political initiative from the Nazis and at the same time satisfy many concerns within the Reichswehr. The militia would absorb jobless young men, provide troops in case of war, and break loose the logjam of promotions for young officers. Chancellor Brüning enthusiastically endorsed the idea and, because both conscription and the creation of an army reserve would violate the Versailles treaty, sought the approval of Britain and France.

Before the Allies responded, however, events overtook Groener's scheme. In October 1931, he was given additional duties as minister of the interior. Now directly responsible for internal order as well as defense, he came under increasing pressure to ban the SA. The powerful provincial governments of Bavaria and Prussia were threatening to take independent action against the Storm Troopers if the national government failed to intervene. By the spring of 1932 Röhm's private army had grown to 400,000 men—four times the size of the Reichswehr—and police raids were turning up evidence that Röhm may have been plotting to use his Storm Troopers in a putsch. These matters were further complicated by a contest for the presidency: The incumbent Hindenburg was being challenged for reelection by Hitler, the upstart whom the eighty-five-year-old field marshal contemptuously dismissed as "that Bohemian corporal."

Groener and the government felt compelled to act. On April 14—three days after President Hindenburg won reelection over Hitler—the cabinet issued a decree banning all uniformed units of the Nazi party, including the Hitler Youth, Hitler's black-shirted SS protection squad, and the SA, because together they formed "a private army whose very existence constitutes a state within the state."

Groener was prepared for the onslaught of protest from the Nazis and extreme nationalists, but not for the reaction within the Reichswehr. Generals who had endorsed suppression of the Storm Troopers now reversed their field. Groener became the target of a smear campaign in his own ministry. He was accused of selling out to the socialists and pacifists; jokes

At Hitler's side, Ernst Röhm, the swashbuckling leader of the SA, salutes his Storm Troopers at a rally in the Berlin Sports Palace. Hitler used Röhm and his men to terrorize rival political parties and whip up enthusiasm for the Nazi cause.

were made about his second marriage at the age of sixty-two and the subsequent arrival of his child.

On May 10, after weathering a storm of invective from the National Socialist benches in the Reichstag, Groener received the worst news of all. His aide and friend, General Kurt von Schleicher, coldly informed him that he "no longer enjoyed the confidence of the army." Three days later, after appealing without avail to his old wartime commander, President Hindenburg, Groener resigned.

The Reichswehr tradition of remaining aloof from politics was now shattered. Many members of the military elite had settled upon the Nazis as the only political party that was both ideologically tolerable and capable

Wilhelm Groener, the most outspoken critic of Hitler in President Hindenburg's cabinet, is satirized in this 1931 cartoon as a fly helplessly entangled in a Nazi spider's web. Within a year, Groener would be hounded from office.

of providing popular support for the kind of authoritarian government the generals envisioned. Moreover, the National Socialists shared the generals' cherished dream of rearmament. As for Adolf Hitler and his lieutenants, they could be disciplined and manipulated. But others caught up in the political fray, the deposed Groener among them, feared that the army's policy of isolation had left the politically naive generals poorly equipped to deal with shrewd performers such as Hitler. A week or so after his resignation, Groener warned a former colleague of the dangers, with this sarcastic reference to Hitler's ancestral name: "It will be up to the generals to see that the army does not in the end kiss Herr Schicklgruber's hands like hysterical women."

Groener's successor as defense minister was his former aide, General Schleicher. Until his appointment, few Germans had even heard of Schleicher, although he had long been one of the most influential figures in the Reichswehr. The son of an aristocratic Brandenburg family, Schleicher

learned early in his military career the value of friends and patrons. In 1900, at the age of eighteen, he joined Hindenburg's old regiment and began a lifelong friendship with the field marshal's son, Oskar. At the War Academy, he studied under Groener and began serving as his aide late in the war. Assigned to Seeckt's staff in the early 1920s, he handled a number of delicate duties, including negotiations with the Russian army for Reichswehr training in the Soviet Union. After Hindenburg's election in 1925, Schleicher was a frequent guest at the presidential palace, where his old friend Oskar served as his father's adjutant.

A colleague of Schleicher in those early days characterized him as "a charming chatterer and wag who got along with everyone. The play behind the curtain suited him better than that before the glaring lamplight of publicity. He was always a clever, not strictly honest, strongly ambitious man with excellent common sense and the tongue to match." Not a few of those who encountered him were reminded that the German word *Schleicher* meant intriguer or sneak.

Schleicher's opportunities for underhandedness grew more frequent after his patron Groener became head of the Defense Ministry. In 1929 Groener appointed him chief liaison with other government ministries and with all the political parties. He called his protégé "my cardinal in politics." During the controversy over the banning of the Nazi troops, Schleicher relied on Groener's trust and his own craftiness to undermine his patron. He planted seeds of doubt in the president's fading mind, lied to leading generals, and started a whispering campaign against Groener. Most devious of all, he met secretly with Röhm and conspired to incorporate the Storm Troopers into the Reichswehr. Later, when Groener learned the extent of Schleicher's treachery, he wrote him: "Scorn and rage boil in me because I have been deceived by you, my old friend, disciple, adopted son, my hope for people and fatherland."

Schleicher saw it differently. He believed that what he had done was for the good of the fatherland. His mission was to rid Germany of political instability by dissolving the Reichstag and replacing it with a cabinet of strong-minded nationalists. Schleicher sought to fulfill his destiny by manipulating politicians of all stripes—even Hitler and the Nazis. He met secretly not only with Röhm but with other party leaders as well, aiming to lure them from Hitler, split the Nazis, and enhance his influence. It was a risky undertaking, as the deposed Groener recognized. "Schleicher relies on his adroitness to lead the Nazis about by the nose," Groener wrote to a friend, "but perhaps they are even more adept than he in the uses of cunning and misrepresentation."

Supremely confident, Schleicher plunged ahead, involving the army

more deeply in politics. Like Groener, who Schleicher believed had become a pawn of the Social Democrats, now Brüning, too, had to go. Schleicher whispered the familiar refrain into the ear of the malleable, aged president—the army had lost confidence in the chancellor. On May 30, scarcely two weeks after Groener's resignation, Brüning was forced out. Nazi leaders watched in wary amusement, and one of them wrote: "Any chancellor who has Herr Schleicher on his side must expect sooner or later to be sunk by the Schleicher torpedo."

At the instigation of Schleicher, who wanted an antidemocratic chancellor, Hindenburg appointed Franz von Papen. A fifty-three-year-old right-wing Westphalian aristocrat best known for his prowess on horseback, Papen had virtually no support in the Reichstag and scant qualifications beyond the considerable charm with which he soon captivated Hindenburg. Schleicher was also allowed to select most members of the new cabinet, which was so dominated by conservative old nobility that it became known as the "cabinet of barons."

Schleicher had cleared his campaign of intrigue with Hitler by early May. In exchange for his acquiescence to Schleicher's scheme for creating a new government, Hitler won promises that the cabinet would lift the ban on Nazi paramilitary organizations, dissolve the Reichstag, and call new elections. The ban was ended on June 16, and Storm Troopers were soon rampaging in the streets again, battling with communists and Social Democrats alike. And in the July elections, the Nazis won 230 seats, more than doubling their parliamentary representation and becoming the largest party in the Reichstag.

Meanwhile, Papen, the chancellor, had made it clear that he intended to rule as a virtual dictator, a startling development that Schleicher could ill afford to tolerate. The defense minister warned the president that Papen's intractable stance threatened to spark a simultaneous revolt by communists and Nazis of such magnitude that the army would not be able to control it. And so, before the end of 1932, Papen was gone—finished off by another Schleicher torpedo.

Schleicher was promoted to chancellor. When he replaced Papen on December 2, while retaining the defense post, his accession marked the apogee of the army's influence in the fourteen-year history of the German republic. Never had the military so dominated the government.

But this power, like the republic itself, was destined for a short life. Schleicher evidently staked everything on a scheme to attract Hitler's main ideological rival in the party, Gregor Strasser, and split the National Socialists. This time his torpedo misfired. Strasser was willing, but Hitler got wind of the intrigue and purged Strasser and his lieutenants from the party.

The accumulating duplicity of Schleicher, meanwhile, finally alienated every faction in the Reichstag—and Hindenburg as well. At the president's behest, Schleicher resigned after only seven weeks as chancellor. Hindenburg then felt compelled to appoint Hitler, whose Nazi party, despite a loss of thirty-four seats in the November elections, still commanded the most votes in the Reichstag.

On January 29, 1933, the eve of the official appointment, Berlin buzzed with rumors that Schleicher and the army high command were plotting a putsch in order to prevent Hitler from assuming power. One story had it that they planned to kidnap the president and establish a military dictatorship. None of it was true. Indeed, Schleicher and his colleagues were so concerned about the chaos that might have erupted had Hitler been denied the position that they contemplated staging an overthrow to make him chancellor. They were convinced in any case that they could make Hitler act as their puppet once he took office.

A new defense minister, Kurt von Schleicher *(right)*, socializes with political rival Franz von Papen, the new chancellor, at a Berlin racetrack in 1932. Schleicher soon engineered Papen's dismissal and became chancellor himself.

But the rumors of an anti-Nazi movement in the army reached the president, and he took unusual precautions. In order to make certain of the army's allegiance, Hindenburg swore in his choice for Schleicher's successor as defense minister early the next morning, a few hours before Hitler's appointment was announced. Hindenberg selected General Werner von Blomberg, a fifty-four-year-old Pomeranian noble and former chief of the general staff, in the belief that Blomberg, unlike Schleicher, exemplified the soldier who remained above politics. Hindenburg, however, could not have been more wrong. Blomberg in fact already was an enthusiastic admirer of Hitler.

The Reichswehr remained obedient—to the president as supreme commander and to the new chancellor and his defense minister. A few days after his appointment, Hitler had dinner with the senior generals and admirals and made some important converts by promising to leave them free for "an undisturbed period" so that they could continue to develop the

A beaming Hitler accepts the plaudits of well-wishers outside the Hotel Kaiserhof after his appointment as chancellor on January 30, 1933. That evening thousands of uniformed supporters celebrated the Nazi triumph with a boisterous torchlit parade through Berlin.

Reich's military capabilities. Even those who still harbored misgivings about the new chancellor felt certain that he could be controlled.

With the army safely in check, Hitler could now devote more time to his campaign to win over Germany's business elite. He had stepped up his efforts in 1931, during the height of the Great Depression, when many disillusioned industrialists were seeking alternatives to a republican government. At the same time Joseph Goebbels and other Nazi propagandists harangued the masses, Hitler traveled the length and breadth of Germany in a big black Mercedes, meeting quietly with magnates of finance and industry. Some of these meetings were so secret, one of Hitler's aides recalled, that they were held "in some lonely forest glade." Privacy was important for both sides in those days: Hitler did not want to be caught hobnobbing with men who were often the targets of National Socialist propaganda, and the titans of business did not want to be publicly associated with Hitler and his radical ideas.

When Hitler spoke to the business owners, he shrewdly told them what they wanted to hear. He focused on themes dear to their economic self-interest, played upon their fears of communism and their dislike of trade unions, and implied that neither would survive under a Nazi government. He assured them that his National Socialists, despite the name, stood for free enterprise. And to the barons of heavy industry, who would benefit most from full-scale rearmament, Hitler hinted of lucrative contracts for weapons and the other paraphernalia of war.

Hitler relied on a network of well-placed agents who provided liaison between the Nazi party and the business community. One of the most influential was Walther Funk, the former editor of a leading financial newspaper. Funk was a homely man—balding, paunchy, and possessed of bulging eyes that reminded the American journalist William L. Shirer of a frog—but he moved in the highest social circles. He joined the party at the urging of industrialists who wanted to influence Nazi economic politics. But he soon became a convert and, like others who had set out to tame the Führer, found himself working for Hitler.

At first, efforts to win over big business failed to enrich Hitler's campaign coffers. He won the outright financial support of only one major capitalist, the steel baron Fritz Thyssen, who as early as 1923 had contributed 100,000 gold marks to the Nazi party. Other industrialists and financiers made token contributions, but only as part of a strategy of hedging their bets by aiding all the major political parties. Some took a page from Schleicher's book and supported potential rivals of Hitler in the hope of splitting the Nazi party or at least influencing its direction.

But Hitler gained from the magnates something more valuable than money: a label of legitimacy that enabled him to take power without active opposition. By January 30, 1933, when he was appointed chancellor, Hitler had succeeded in convincing the business community as well as the army that he was a viable alternative for Germany's political future. Business people were willing to wait and see. For many, the Nazi program seemed preferable to the political and economic chaos afflicting their country, and in any event, they—like many of the generals—were certain that Hitler could eventually be made to do their bidding.

Once in power, Hitler sought to consolidate his links to industry and to exploit them. On February 20, three weeks after his appointment, about twenty leading industrialists gathered at the Berlin residence of Hermann Göring, the Führer's right-hand man and president of the Reichstag. The occasion was a Nazi fund-raiser for the election to be held the following month, and in his ninety-minute speech, Hitler struck all the right chords. "All the benefits of culture," he intoned, "must be introduced more or less with an iron fist." Both industry and the army, he expounded, must be restored to their lost brilliance. Hitler finished with a rousing crescendo and made a sweeping exit, and the assembled tycoons dutifully arose to pledge their financial support. One of the first on his feet was Germany's best-known industrialist and arms maker, Gustav Krupp, who joined the others in a pledge of three million reichsmarks for Hitler and the greater glory of the new German Reich.

The conversion of Krupp represented a major coup. Krupp had been wary of Hitler for many reasons. Not the least of these was that the Führer had been a lowly corporal, and Krupp was accustomed to socializing with generals such as Hans von Seeckt and Kurt von Schleicher. Krupp also liked to think of himself as above politics, and he forbade discussion of the subject in his home. His unqualified loyalty was to the state, no matter who was in power. Though instinctively a monarchist, his reverence for chiefs of state was so great that he once stalked indignantly from a meeting when a fellow industrialist referred to the late socialist president, Friedrich Ebert, as "that saddle maker."

But as the depression deepened, Krupp became disenchanted with the republic. In the Krupp Works at Essen, where fewer than half of the smokestacks now poured out sooty brown smoke, an American journalist on a tour saw an inactive steel press "sticking out of the cold mouth of a furnace like a half-chewed match. Heavy with idleness, it was Germany today. Potent, it was Germany tomorrow." By 1932 Krupp's work force at the main plant, formerly 40,000 laborers, had been reduced to 18,000 part-time employees. Profits plummeted so low that Krupp and his family were compelled to cut their living expenses; they closed the main part of their palatial Villa Hügel and made do in a mere sixty rooms.

Hounded by the depression, Krupp began to pay attention to the National Socialists early in 1932. He dispatched a member of his board of directors to hear Hitler address a blue-ribbon audience at the Industry Club in Düsseldorf; the emissary was so impressed he returned spouting Nazi propaganda. Krupp's eldest son, Alfried, had already succumbed to nazism the previous year, joining Heinrich Himmler's black-shirted SS as a sponsoring member while still a twenty-four-year-old college student. Gustav Krupp gave money to the Nazi party, but only as part of his policy of contributing to all the right-wing parties. Krupp was not easily wooed, according to the industrialist Thyssen. "As late as the day before President Hindenburg appointed Adolf Hitler chancellor," Thyssen wrote, "Krupp urgently warned the old field marshal against such a course."

Even after he met the new chancellor for the first time at Göring's house and endorsed the Nazis with his financial pledge, Krupp evidently had reservations. Still unsure of the correct political path, he wanted to keep his options open. For example, Krupp issued precise instructions to Karl Stahl, his Berlin chauffeur, on how to salute him. Krupp's gloves would be the signal. If Krupp carried them in his right hand, Stahl was to click his heels and touch the bill of his cap in the time-honored Prussian salute. If the gloves were in Krupp's left hand, Stahl was to raise his right arm stiffly so that the chauffeur and magnate could exchange Hitler's new form of acknowledgment.

It was not long, however, before Krupp made a firm decision. The turning point in his personal political quandary was the March national election. The Nazis won 44 percent of the vote and, with money donated by Krupp

Steel magnate Fritz Thyssen *(right)*, an early Hitler supporter, talks with propaganda chief Goebbels at an economic conference in 1933. Hitler, declared Thyssen, "is the only man who can and will rescue Germany from ruin and disgrace."

and other industrialists, coerced enough additional Reichstag members to push through the so-called Enabling Act, which gave Hitler dictatorial authority. Now the person of the Führer and the concept of the German state merged in Krupp's mind, and the formerly cautious industrialist threw his loyalty to the Nazi party without reservation. He became—in Thyssen's words—"a super Nazi."

His first chores on behalf of the Führer were as chief fund-raiser for the party. In this post, he devised a clever scheme known as the Hitler *Spende*, or fund, for dipping into the pockets of his fellow businessmen. A donor's contribution, said Krupp, amounted to "a token of gratitude to the leader of the nation." But as the donors realized from the outset, it was also protection money. Certification as a donor brought immunity from harassment by Storm Troopers and other party thugs financed by the fund. Krupp himself contributed more than six million reichsmarks to the Hitler Spende and an equivalent amount to other Nazi causes.

Through Krupp, Hitler was able to institutionalize the new alliance between big business and National Socialism. The two men agreed to convert the Federation of German Industries, a trade association that Krupp had headed since 1931, into a quasi-official agency. Krupp remained the chief, but with a new designation as Führer of German industry. Krupp quickly lived up to that imperious title by expelling all the Jewish members of the trade association, dissolving its board of directors, and banning any further meetings without his consent.

At the same time, Krupp grew more assertive in his own industrial realm. In August 1933, six months after Hitler took office, Krupp made the Nazi salute compulsory not only in his own factories but in other German industries as well. He instructed his sales representatives abroad to disseminate propaganda about the "new Germany" and later enlisted them as part-time members of the Reich's espionage network. At the Essen works, he maintained a special telephone link with the local headquarters of the new secret police, the Gestapo. Employees who criticized the Nazi regime were sent there for questioning. Many did not come back; indeed, hundreds of Krupp employees wound up in concentration camps. Krupp brushed aside concerns about such inhumanity with the old German saying "Where there is planing, shavings fall."

Bertha Krupp watched with misgivings as her husband slipped into Hitler's thrall. A woman of the very highest social station whose family had always associated with royalty, she could not bear to even utter Hitler's name. She referred to him as "that certain gentleman." When the Nazi flag replaced that of imperial Germany on the poles in front of their castle, she snapped to her maid, "Go in the park and see how low we have fallen."

Munitions tycoon Gustav Krupp (*standing at right*) commissioned this family painting to celebrate his wedding anniversary in 1931. His wife Bertha (*at Krupp's right*) was contemptuous of Hitler. She owned the business, but her pro-Nazi husband controlled it.

Bertha pleaded a headache when Hitler paid his first official visit to the Krupp Works in June 1934. Krupp's eldest daughter, twenty-one-year-old Irmgard, filled in as hostess. She gave Hitler flowers and a curtsy. He smiled in appreciation and then hugged her father. It was not Hitler's first visit to the works. He had appeared at the gate there in 1929 and demanded a tour of the plant but had been turned away. Krupp had feared that the little-known Nazi agitator might see some of the secret rearmament work going on inside and reveal it to the outside world.

Hitler pandered to the interests of Krupp and others in business in myriad ways, one of which was the brutal suppression of organized labor and its political allies—a campaign carried out under the slogan "the public interest before selfish interest." He clamped on wage controls and abolished the eight-hour workday in order to eliminate premium pay for overtime. He banned all trade unions and the Social Democratic party, outlawed strikes and collective bargaining, and imprisoned many labor leaders.

The business community also benefited greatly from new government spending policies that brought rapid economic recovery and virtually full employment by 1936. A combination of reduced taxes and various grants

and subsidies to farmers, small businesses, and heavy industry injected new purchasing power into the economy. So too did vastly increased government spending for construction, road building, and other public-works projects, outlays that tripled from 9 billion reichsmarks in 1933 to almost 30 billion in 1938.

The rearmament projects ordered by Hitler solidified the industrialists' alliance with the Führer. Krupp had a head start, of course. As the only major industrialist to defy the Versailles treaty during the 1920s, he was already gearing up for production. By the end of April of 1933, only three months after Hitler had become chancellor, Krupp was stockpiling scrap iron, iron ore, copper, and other raw materials at rates that were up to eight times those of the previous year. Krupp wrote later: "I had the satisfaction of being able to report to the Führer that Krupp stood ready, after a short warming-up period, to begin the rearmament of the German people without any gaps in our experience. In the years after 1933, we worked with incredible intenseness."

Krupp's entire industrial empire thrived. At the Krawa truck plant, the assembly line retooled for the production of tanks—Hitler wanted 100 light tanks by March of 1934 and 650 more a year later. At Essen thousands of blocks of steel that had been cast in earlier years were molded into gun barrels; the work force there quickly tripled, and steel production more than doubled within a year. At Kiel construction of submarines, destroyers, and minesweepers began behind immense screens intended to shield the activity from outside eyes.

During that first year of covert rearmament under Hitler, the Krupp firm signed no formal contracts with the government but merely relied on the spoken commitments of high-ranking Reichswehr ordnance officers. Nonetheless, in 1933 the company started making profits again, and the annual take rose astronomically—to 97 million reichsmarks by 1938. Thanks to the rearmament policies of "that certain gentleman" in Berlin, Bertha Krupp now could afford to move her family back into the main section of Villa Hügel.

Hitler was not yet prepared to publicly reveal these violations of the Versailles treaty, although he was inching in that direction. In October 1933, for example, he pulled Germany out of the European Disarmament Conference and withdrew from the League of Nations. But he continued to conceal rearmament operations, including his first arms budget.

Hitler's success in maintaining financial secrecy stemmed largely from the wizardry of his economics expert, Horace Greeley Hjalmar Schacht. The son of a German who had emigrated to the United States during the 1870s and then returned to the fatherland, Schacht was named after the dynamic editor of the New York *Tribune*, a man his father greatly admired. As president of the German national bank during the 1920s, Schacht devised the policy of issuing new currency that was backed by foreign loans; his strategy stabilized the mark and braked Germany's runaway inflation. Politically a maverick who soon soured on parliamentary democracy, he became enamored of National Socialism and served the Nazi regime not only as bank president but also as economics minister and then plenipotentiary general for the war economy.

Schacht secretly financed rearmament with a special kind of IOU. Krupp and other arms contractors were paid not in marks but in certificates that were known as Mefo bills. The contractor could use them instead of currency to purchase raw materials and other necessities. Banks or private investors then held the bills for five years, after which they were redeemable by a government holding company from whose name the acronym *Mefo*

Financial expert Hjalmar Schacht *(center)*, seeking American support for a moratorium on German debt payments, visits President Franklin D. Roosevelt in May of 1933. Roosevelt took office in March, five weeks after Hitler had become chancellor.

Hitler breaks ground in September 1933 for a section of the autobahn between Frankfurt and Darmstadt. He publicized his acceleration of the highway-building program as an "overture to peace"—although a major reason for it was to speed troops and supplies across Germany.

was derived. All the transactions occurred without one of the billions of marks spent for rearmament actually appearing on the record. Many of the Mefo bills were redeemed with funds confiscated from foreign accounts and from Jews and others considered enemies of the state. "Thus," Schacht reported proudly to War Minister Blomberg in 1936, "our armaments are partially financed with the credits of our political enemies."

In addition to the production of actual weapons, Hitler planned the development of an infrastructure to support rearmament. In 1933, for example, he launched construction of a network of efficient *Autobahnen*, or highways, that were designed to link German cities. The paving and use of these new highways stimulated the economy—and hence strengthened Hitler's position with members of the business community. Just as important, the roads would permit the swift movement of the army's tanks and trucks in case of war.

Even more vital to the Reich's military fortunes was the development of adequate supplies of gasoline, rubber, and other essential substances. Traditionally, Germany had to import the raw materials that went into every drop of gasoline and each ounce of rubber. It was this dependence on strategic materials from abroad that decisively weakened Germany during the First World War, when the naval blockade erected by Great Britain slowly strangled the flow of imports. Hitler was determined to avoid the same fate by creating synthetics that would make the Reich and its armed forces self-sufficient.

Germany's leading company in the development of synthetics—indeed, its largest corporation of any kind—was the chemical giant known as I. G. Farben. The firm was created in 1925 by the merger of eight companies that manufactured synthetic dyes from coal tar, a by-product of steel production in the Ruhr. The company name often confounded foreign researchers who sought in vain to identify an industrialist by that name. *I. G. Farben* was actually an acronym derived from the corporation's German name: *Interessen Gemeinschaft der deutschen Teerfarbenindustrie*, or the Community of Interest of the German Dyestuff Industry.

Well before the merger, I. G. Farben's predecessor companies had made vital contributions to German arms. During World War I their researchers had achieved two technological breakthroughs: the development of poison gases and the mass production of a synthetic form of nitrate, a substance essential for making gunpowder and other explosives. Synthetic nitrates had enabled Germany to survive the loss of its supply of naturally occurring nitrate, saltpeter imported from the mines of Chile.

The man most responsible for the production of synthetic nitrates—and for the merger of the I. G. Farben companies—was Carl Bosch. A gifted executive and scientist trained in both organic chemistry and metallurgical engineering, Bosch had enlarged on the achievement of another German scientist, Fritz Haber, a university researcher. Before the war Haber had invented a process through which ammonia was synthesized under high pressures from nitrogen and hydrogen; ammonia could easily be used to make nitrates. Bosch took Haber's invention from the laboratory to the factory and perfected the mass-production processes.

In 1925 Bosch proposed the I. G. Farben merger. He realized that the combined resources of the eight companies offered hope for incredible profits—and for liberation of Germany from dependence on foreign oil. The

key to these goals was extracting oil and gasoline from coal. As early as 1909 one of Haber's assistants, Friedrich Bergius, had succeeded in converting a slurry of powdered coal and oil to pure petroleum by introducing hydrogen under high pressure. Although Germany possessed coal in great abundance, no one had made oil from it in this way outside the laboratory. Determined to repeat his earlier success, Bosch pushed through the merger, became chairman of the managing board of I. G. Farben, and purchased the Bergius patents. In late 1926, less than a year after the creation of the company, he was ready to undertake construction at Leuna of the world's first plant for the mass production of synthetic oil. For this and his earlier engineering achievement with nitrates, Bosch in 1931 would share with Bergius the Nobel Prize in chemistry.

The plant at Leuna could produce up to 100,000 tons of gasoline and other fuels and lubricants annually. But a huge obstacle loomed, and that was cost. Making synthetic fuels from coal was prohibitively more expensive than refining crude oil, the traditional method. The disparity grew even greater during the Great Depression, when the price of crude oil dropped precipitously. Bosch negotiated a joint venture with the American giant, Standard Oil of New Jersey, to apply the Bergius process to crude oil and thus double the efficiency of conventional refining. But the plummeting price of crude made even that variation too costly. By 1930 a liter of synthetic gasoline cost up to seven times as much as the traditionally refined fuel, and several members of Bosch's board of directors wanted to abandon the Leuna operation.

Anxious to secure government support, I. G. Farben plunged deeper into the political arena. The company gave money to all the major parties except the extremists—communists and Nazis—and even subsidized a newspaper, the *Frankfurter Zeitung*, as a voice that spoke for democracy and, not coincidentally, for the virtues of synthetic oil. The company contributed so much to the campaign treasury of Heinrich Brüning that he became known as the "I. G. chancellor." It paid off: In 1931 the government backed a stiff tariff on imported oil. Passed the following year, the tax enabled I. G. Farben to enter the domestic market with synthetic gasoline.

In 1932 the company began financing the Nazis as well. The motives were twofold: to silence the scurrilous attacks in the Nazi press on the company's Jewish directors and to ensure the party's backing for synthetic fuel. Late that year, after the Nazis attained dominance in the Reichstag, Bosch sent two representatives to Munich to sound out Hitler. The I. G. Farben men were pleasantly surprised by Hitler's enthusiasm for German self-sufficiency in petroleum and by his "amazing understanding for technical matters," as one of them put it. When they reported to Bosch that

Giant ammonia-storage tanks dwarf two workers on a catwalk at the I. G. Farben nitrogen plant in Leuna, Germany. The factory, one of 900 owned by the chemical cartel, produced synthetic nitrates used in the manufacture of explosives.

Hitler had assured them of his support when he came to power, Bosch commented, "The man is more sensible than I thought."

Bosch had reason to think otherwise a few months later, when he met the Führer for the first time. Hitler was now chancellor, and they got along amicably so long as the subject of conversation was synthetic oil. But Bosch brought up a matter that his colleagues had urged him to avoid. Concerned about the fate of Jewish scientists who were being forced from their jobs and out of Germany, Bosch warned Hitler that expulsion of Jewish physicists and chemists would stall German progress in the sciences for a century. "Then we'll work a hundred years without physics and chemistry!" roared Hitler. With that, the Führer abruptly brought the meeting to an end and refused thereafter to appear in the same room with the chairman of the board of I. G. Farben.

Rolls of synthetic rubber called Buna, invented by German scientists, fill an I. G. Farben warehouse. The technological breakthrough helped Germany attain the self-sufficiency that Hitler needed in order to maneuver in world politics.

Undeterred by Hitler's hostility, Bosch continued his campaign on behalf of Jewish scientists with much courage but little success. A few weeks after his meeting with Hitler, Bosch learned that his old colleague Haber had been dismissed from his post at Berlin University. Haber lost his job even though he was a longtime convert to Christianity, a winner of the Nobel Prize in chemistry, and, through his work on both synthetic ammonia and poison gases, a major contributor to military rearmament. Haber died in Swiss exile in January 1934, a broken man but not a forgotten one. On the first anniversary of his death, Bosch defied the Nazis by organizing a memorial ceremony that was attended by more than 500 persons, including many of Haber's high-ranking army friends.

However, the mutual needs of the two strong-willed antagonists—Hitler's for synthetic oil and Bosch's for government aid to produce it—overcame their personal antipathy. Representatives of Bosch and the Führer signed a formal agreement on December 14, 1933. In return for a government pledge to guarantee a price sufficient to cover all production costs plus some profit, I. G. Farben agreed to enlarge its plant at Leuna during the next four years in order to triple the current annual output of 100,000 tons of synthetic petroleum.

With the nation's oil problem apparently solved, attention was directed toward another synthetic material that was essential for motorizing the German military: a substitute for natural rubber. Research in synthetic rubber by I. G. Farben's predecessors dating from World War I had resulted in the production of several thousand tons of a material too hard and inelastic for use in tires. During the late 1920s the company settled on a more versatile synthetic called Buna, which was first manufactured from coal and later from oil. The name *Buna* was formed by joining the initial syllables of the words *butadiene*, the hydrocarbon, and *natrium*, the German word for sodium, the two materials used to make the first version. Like synthetic oil, Buna could not compete with the real thing in the marketplace without subsidies from the government. Hitler's finance chief, Schacht, dragged his feet on the issue, but Hitler intervened and gave guarantees to I. G. Farben. The company began construction of the first of four synthetic-rubber factories in 1936.

Relations between Hitler and his indispensable supplier of synthetics meanwhile took a smoother turn with the progressive nazification of I. G. Farben. In 1935 the maverick Bosch retired to a largely honorary position. His successor as board chairman, as well as other top company officials, joined the Nazi party and soon purged Farben's board and executive ranks of all Jews. Bosch went into mental and physical decline and died in 1940, brooding at the end that his epic achievements—the mass production

of synthetic nitrates, oil, and rubber—had not only provided for the nation's defense but had enabled Adolf Hitler to launch an unjust war.

As German industry pushed toward rearmament with new vigor, Hitler sought to strengthen his ties to the army. He worked skillfully to win over the generals who had stood by without enthusiasm when he took office. He gained many new adherents by stepping up arms production and allowing the Reichswehr to both ignore the 100,000-man limit imposed by the Versailles treaty and implement plans for tripling its personnel by 1935. He also won favor by treating the generals with unfailing courtesy and respect and offering fulsome public praise for the old soldier, President Hindenburg. In January 1934, speaking on his first anniversary as chancellor, he went so far as to rank the army as one of the "two pillars" of the Reich; the other pillar, of course, was the Nazi party.

Many senior officers were impressed, too, by the way Hitler kept his hands off promotions and otherwise refrained from meddling in the army's internal affairs. The Führer could afford this luxury because he trusted his defense minister, General Werner von Blomberg, to handle such matters. Although Blomberg had been Hindenburg's choice, Hitler quickly warmed to him. Tall, handsome—a commanding presence in the immaculate uniform that he continued to wear in the technically civilian post—Blomberg proved himself a capable administrator and an ardent acolyte of Hitler. "The Führer is cleverer than we are," he told his generals. "He will plan and do everything correctly."

Acting on his own, Blomberg gradually introduced nazism and its trappings into the army and navy. He ordered all servicemen to salute uniformed members of the party, and he institutionalized the Hitler salute. He tinkered with army insignia on tunics and caps, inserting the Nazi swastika into the claws of the old imperial army's traditional eagle. He purged the ranks of the few remaining Jews (excepting those who were war veterans), forbade shopping in Jewish-owned stores, and banned marriages to Jews. Few in the Reichswehr saw fit to protest; after all, as a historian later observed, the army "had never been the champion of civil liberties, Jews, socialism, or democracy."

One unresolved issue clouded the atmosphere of growing trust between Hitler and the Reichswehr. The SA was burgeoning in size and power. The Storm Troopers now numbered nearly three million men, and their chief Ernst Röhm sat in the cabinet as a minister without portfolio. Röhm scorned the generals as "a lot of old fogeys" and openly advocated an outrageous plan for his SA to absorb the Reichswehr and create a huge "people's army"—presumably under his command. Hitler rejected Röhm's

Recruits of the Regiment General Göring, a former police unit formed in 1933 to suppress any remaining challenge to the Nazi party, pledge allegiance to Hitler. When he took over the government, Hitler ordered all military personnel to swear an oath of fealty to him personally.

ambitions and repeatedly reassured the generals that the Reichswehr would be "the sole bearer of arms" in his Reich. But the generals were not mollified. They saw the Brownshirts as a threat to their military monopoly and viewed Röhm and his disreputable associates as nothing less than menaces to morality and the rejuvenation of Germany. "Rearmament," one leading general later remarked, "was too serious and difficult a business to permit the participation of peculators, drunkards, and homosexuals."

The issue came to a climax late in June 1934, when disparate pressures converged on Hitler. Blomberg and the army leadership kept up a drumbeat of complaints about the SA. Industrialists such as Krupp, concerned about SA violence, added their objections. Two of Hitler's closest Nazi subordinates, Hermann Göring, chief of the new Air Ministry, and Heinrich Himmler of the SS, wanted him to move against Röhm in order to rid the party of a rival faction. Röhm was now openly scornful of Hitler, referring to him as "that ridiculous corporal." More important, the eighty-seven-year-old Hindenburg lay near death; when he died Hitler intended to name himself president, and he needed the Reichswehr on his side.

Hitler finally acted after Göring and Himmler convinced him that the Storm Troopers intended to mount a putsch against his regime. Before dawn on June 30, Himmler's SS men began the purge. The army was spared the indignity of direct participation but did provide the Blackshirts with rifles, ammunition, and transportation. During the next forty-eight hours, Himmler's assassins eliminated not only Röhm and his associates but also dozens of others who had been deemed enemies of the regime. Among the dead were two retired generals: Kurt von Schleicher, the former defense minister and chancellor, and Ferdinand von Bredow, his onetime subordinate. Both were shot, the official story went, while resisting arrest for treasonable activities.

In the official view of the Reichswehr, Hitler had performed admirably. Defense Minister Blomberg issued an order of the day that extolled the Führer for his "soldierly resoluteness and exemplary courage" in ridding the Reich of "traitors and mutineers." Only the persistence and courage of a small collection of officers, including retired General Kurt von Hammerstein, the Reichswehr's commander under Schleicher, redeemed a fragment of the army's tattered integrity. Hammerstein and the others mounted such a relentless campaign to remove the stain of dishonor from Schleicher and Bredow that Hitler was forced to embroider the lie with further falsehood: Schleicher and Bredow had been killed in error, the Führer told his senior commanders, and their names should be restored to the honor rolls of their respective regiments.

A month after the purge, Hitler was able to complete his subjugation of the army. On August 2, 1934, Hindenburg died, and Hitler proclaimed himself successor by merging the offices of president and chancellor and assuming supreme command of the armed forces. That afternoon, even as the army and the nation mourned the old soldier, Blomberg ordered the officers and enlisted men of the Reichswehr to take a new oath. Instead of vowing their allegiance to the constitution of Germany, as had been the practice under the republic, they swore loyalty to the head of state, as in the prewar days of the empire. They pledged "unconditional obedience to the Führer of the German Reich and people, Adolf Hitler, the supreme commander of the armed forces."

It remained for the Führer to redeem in full his longstanding pledge to the generals: the restoration of Germany's military might. The following spring, on March 16, 1935, Hitler publicly decreed the rebirth of universal conscription and ordered that the army—already 280,000 men strong—be increased by another eight divisions. Trumpets and drums resounded throughout the Reich. No longer would Germany rearm in secret. Hitler had thrown off the shackles of Versailles. ✚

Backed by a Wehrmacht color guard, General Werner von Blomberg, Hitler's first minister of defense and supreme commander of the armed forces, delivers a speech at the Kroll Opera House. The appointment of Blomberg, a respected professional soldier, ended any temptation on the part of high-ranking officers to rebel against the new regime.

A Symbolic Union of Warriors and the Party

"The armed forces stand in close unity with the whole nation," wrote Defense Minister Werner von Blomberg, "wearing with pride the symbol of Germany's rebirth." That new symbol was a traditional German eagle, now clutching in its talons the swastika of the Nazi party. On February 25, 1934, thousands of German soldiers, sailors, and airmen had been ordered to stitch the emblem onto the right breast of their uniform coats and pin it to their hats and caps.

The union of the German military with Hitler's year-old regime was further celebrated when the rearmed and expanded Wehrmacht unveiled a host of uniform styles. The youngest branch of service, the Luftwaffe, adopted the designs of its predecessor organization, the German Air Sports League. The army and navy retained some existing styles, modified others, and designed distinctive lines of formal dress. They also combined pieces from discrete uniforms and added fresh insignia and accouterments.

The permutations proliferated, and by 1938 an army officer might possess as many as ten different configurations—including parade uniform, service dress, field uniform, and sports dress, all worn in various combinations for occasions that ranged from attending maneuvers to calling upon a senior officer in his headquarters. Published booklets of regulations carefully spelled out which uniform was to be worn for a specific activity.

Following the example of the National Socialists, daggers were introduced for undress, or semiformal, wear for officers of the army and Luftwaffe. As a further sign of the union of military and party, certain political and Freikorps decorations, which had been forbidden during the Weimar era, were now permitted to be worn with the uniform.

An army officer's tunic and cap were worn on full-dress occasions. Collar and shoulder insignia indicated rank and branch of service— in this case, a second lieutenant of the Parachute Infantry Battalion. Officers of all ranks wore the aiguillettes and brocade belt.

The cap and field-service tunic of a cavalry officer, with an army officer's dagger, were intended as an undress uniform for dismounted duty. The field-service tunic was produced with and without piping; which version was worn depended on the degree of formality required.

The model 1936 field-service tunic was loose-fitting enough to be comfortable in combat but tailored at the waist for a smart appearance. This example belonged to a sergeant in Machine-Gun Battalion 5; it was worn in the field with the 1916 steel helmet or the 1938 field cap.

This tunic and cap were designed for the Luftwaffe in 1935. The model 1937 Luftwaffe officer's dagger was suspended from the Sam Browne belt on undress occasions. The same tunic, with different appointments, was worn for full dress.

The *Fliegerbluse*, or airman's blouse, inspired by the German army's 1915 field jacket, was issued to all ranks. The jacket shown here, along with the officer's forage cap piped in silver, was worn by a second lieutenant qualified as a pilot. The 1935 aviator's dagger was patterned after a design from the German Air Sports League.

This service tunic, owned by a private in the 86th Flak Artillery Regiment, could be worn on parade along with the model 1935 steel helmet and field accouterments. The helmet bears the Luftwaffe's distinctive eagle decal. The forage cap, worn with less formal attire, lacks the officer's silver piping shown at top.

Except for its Nazi eagle,
this commander's reefer was
identical to the standard undress
jacket worn by most of the
world's naval officers. The sleeve
braid and the oak leaves on the
visor of the service cap indicate
rank. The dirk was the same
as the Imperial Navy pattern,
but a swastika on the pommel
replaced the old eagle emblem.

The addition of gold epaulets converted this lieutenant's frock coat from service dress to full dress. A cocked hat was substituted for the service cap *(above right)* on such occasions.

The peacoat *(far left)* was worn outdoors in cold weather by all naval ratings. The uniform jacket *(left)* was worn over the standard jumper for dress events. The traditional sailor's caps were either white for summer or blue for winter, and ships' names were embroidered in gold wire on the ribbon. All German naval ratings' uniforms bore double insignia on the left sleeve; the top designated the wearer's rank, the bottom his specialty.

Prophets of a New Kind of Warfare

Early in 1934, toward the end of his first turbulent year as ruler of the German nation, Adolf Hitler attended an unusual military demonstration. Accompanied by his boisterous confidant, Hermann Göring, and his dour defense minister, Werner von Blomberg, Hitler took a half hour from his schedule to appraise the radical ideas of a forty-five-year-old lieutenant colonel who believed he had discovered a new way to fight a war. Soldiers of the old school must have been mystified by the exercise that unfolded before the Führer's eyes at the army training ground at Kunersdorf. Instead of cavalry, motorcycles and armored cars buzzed across the landscape scouting enemy positions. A handful of ungainly tanks—little two-man vehicles, each armed only with a couple of machine guns—advanced toward the enemy line, accompanied by antitank guns towed by trucks. Nowhere to be seen were the traditional ranks of troops pushing forward from their trenches behind an artillery barrage.

Not only was Lieutenant Colonel Heinz Guderian proposing to use armor as the attacking force in future campaigns, he was insisting that the entire German army be reorganized to incorporate his plan, and that the country's industries mobilize to implement it. It seemed an improbable notion in a nation still constrained by the harsh terms of the Versailles treaty and hampered by the effects of the worldwide depression.

The implications of Guderian's theories could not have pleased Göring. As air minister, his priorities lay elsewhere. He was presiding over an ambitious program of aerial rearmament. Employment in the aircraft industry had quadrupled in a single year, production of aircraft had more than doubled, and progressive new designs for fighters, bombers, and reconnaissance planes were on the drawing boards. The immensity of the program had strained the financial resources of the government and the manufacturing capacity of the country.

But Hitler—not Göring—had the final word on Guderian's proposal. And Hitler was delighted with the colonel's unorthodox concept of armor as the front-line force. "That's what I need!" exclaimed the enthusiastic Führer. "That's what I want!" In Hitler's Germany, such a remark could have

A squadron of He 51 fighters flies over an 88-mm antiaircraft gun in an aerial display. After Hitler publicly acknowledged the existence of the Luftwaffe in 1935, German air power was flaunted on state occasions.

far-reaching consequences for a man's career, as Göring knew very well—
and as Guderian was about to discover.

Change was in the air everywhere in Germany at the midpoint of the
1930s, but nowhere was it more pronounced than in the armed forces. Just
fifteen years after the Allies at Versailles sentenced Germany to a seemingly
permanent state of military inferiority, Hitler was prodding his strategists
to restore the nation's capacity to wage war on a major scale. And Hitler
was prepared to risk far more, far sooner, than anyone yet suspected.

The difficulty of the task was compounded by the breakneck pace of
postwar technological change. Most generals simply could not keep up.
Military panels were wrangling over how to reconcile the traditional role
of the cavalry with the brutal efficiency of the machine gun and tank. The
capabilities of aircraft, motor vehicles, ships, submarines, and such vital
ancillaries as radio and radar were increasing at dizzying speeds. Airplane
designs were becoming obsolete while still on the drawing board.

Officers of a younger generation were arguing that the basic doctrines
of warfare must be reshaped to accommodate the new technology. In 1934,
with the engines of rearmament revving up, these prophets of a new
warfare were trying desperately, with varying success, to change the thinking of their services.

In the Air Ministry, Göring's chief of staff Walther Wever and others
preached the need for an autonomous, strategic air force to an audience

Hitler and Göring lead senior officers across a wind-swept airfield at Döberitz in 1935 to inspect the new Richthofen Squadron. The squadron's pilots had trained in civilian flying clubs before they donned the Luftwaffe's blue-gray uniform.

Walther Wever, the Luftwaffe's brilliant first chief of staff, pushed the development of a long-range strategic bomber. But Wever died in a plane crash in 1936, and his test program was severely curtailed.

of largely indifferent, aging fighter pilots and recently transferred infantry officers. In the army, Guderian championed the theory that caught Hitler's fancy: Armored units, linked by radio, would bring to bear what Guderian called "decisive force." The proposal encountered stiff resistance from officers firmly rooted in the doctrines of trench warfare. And in the navy, Captain Karl Dönitz, a veteran U-boat commander, espoused a new way to use the submarine and insisted that it, not the battleship, would be the decisive weapon in any future conflict.

The driving force behind the growth of German air power was Hermann Göring, chief of the Air Ministry. He possessed vast ambition and energy and could count on the ardent support of leading figures in Germany's booming aviation industry, having represented their interests in the Reichstag before the Nazis came to power. And he was prized by his Führer for other reasons. In addition to the prerequisites for membership in Hitler's inner circle—unstinting loyalty and the absence of any ethical compunctions—Göring offered an attribute that was rare among Hitler's cronies: He was an authentic war hero.

The son of a prominent German colonial official, Göring went to war in 1914 as a twenty-one-year-old infantry lieutenant. The following year he transferred to the Flying Corps, where he distinguished himself, shooting

down fifteen enemy aircraft by 1917 and winning the coveted Prussian order Pour le mérite, known as the Blue Max. In 1918 he succeeded to the command of Jagd Geschwader 1, the late Manfred von Richthofen's celebrated squadron—the one the Allies called the Flying Circus. Outraged when Germany agreed to an armistice that November, Göring told the men of his squadron in parting: "We will fight against these forces that are seeking to enslave us, and will win through. Our time will come again."

A few years later, after touring Scandinavia as a taxi pilot and stunt flier and marrying a baron's daughter, Göring met the man who

Members of the SA solicit donations to their flying club during an Aviation Week campaign in 1933. The club was later absorbed into the Luftwaffe.

would lead him in the new fight. Göring's assets were immediately apparent to Hitler. "A war ace with the Pour le mérite—imagine it!" Hitler remarked shortly after meeting him in Munich. "Moreover, he has money and doesn't cost me a cent!" The Führer also appreciated Göring's entrée into an arena where Hitler would always be an outsider—the drawing rooms and dinner tables of the country's industrialists and financiers. Göring, for his part, regarded Hitler as Germany's savior and never lost his reverential awe of the man. "Every time I see him," Göring confessed to Economics Minister Hjalmar Schacht, "my heart falls into my trousers."

Göring's devotion to Hitler and his manifest talent for political maneuvering brought him immediate rewards when the Nazis came to power early in 1933. He was named minister of the interior for Prussia, Germany's largest state, and organized a secret police force there—the Gestapo—whose sinister efficiency would become legendary. Yet he remained obsessed with the future of German air power, and his appointment as chief of the Reich's new Air Ministry in May was a dream fulfilled.

To be sure, the science of aviation had advanced dramatically since Göring last flew in combat. His experience with postwar aviation had been limited to business contacts that had hardly prepared him to fathom such technological developments as supercharged engines, streamlined alloy hulls, and pressurized cabins. He was convinced, however, that aviation was the wave of the future and that Germany should develop a strong, independent air force. Toward that objective he turned his considerable intelligence and infectious enthusiasm.

Göring's first concern was to consolidate his authority. With Hitler's backing, he succeeded in organizing the air forces of the army and navy as a separate service under his exclusive command. "Everything that flies," he would soon boast, "belongs to me!" For personnel, he had at his disposal an elite cadre of pilots who had been trained in military aviation in Russia and who stood ready to lead any mobilization. There were 15,000 glider pilots and 1,000 airplane pilots in the country's 300 private, paramilitary flying clubs, all of which were lumped by Göring into the mammoth German Air Sports League. The country had about 100 good airfields in daily use, an array of excellent weather stations, and a network of radio communications. In addition, Germany possessed Lufthansa, one of the best and biggest airlines in the world. Lufthansa was flying more miles and carrying more passengers than the French, British, and Italian airlines combined, and its pilots and many of its aircraft could be quickly converted to military applications.

But Göring's program of aerial rearmament still faced serious problems. Although planning for a new German air force had been proceeding in secret for more than a decade, it was 1932 before the aircraft industry at last met the requirements for four military-aircraft prototypes—two reconnaissance planes, a fighter, and a bomber. And there were indications that Germany might never be able to produce enough aircraft. When Göring took over the Air Ministry, he had to reckon with the disturbing conclusions of a recent study conducted by Lieutenant Colonel Hellmuth Felmy, chief of air operations and training. Felmy calculated that in order to wage war effectively, Germany would need 1,056 aircraft in eighty squadrons—twenty reconnaissance, eighteen fighter, and forty-two bomber squadrons. And in a chilling advisory, he estimated that in an all-out war this air force would lose half of its planes per month.

The realists in industry and the military were appalled. Despite massive government subsidies, the country possessed only a fraction of the materials and the manufacturing capacity needed to meet such staggering requirements. There were 3,200 people at work in seven major airframe factories and four engine plants, but most aircraft were still custom-built, each laboriously completed before the next was begun. Only two firms, Junkers and Heinkel, were capable of mass production, and Junkers—along with Dornier—was in serious financial trouble. Under emergency conditions, the industry could probably turn out 100 single-engine aircraft per month, or one-fifth the wartime demand projected by Felmy.

To spur the aircraft industry, Göring looked to Erhard Milch, the managing director of Lufthansa. Milch, forty-one years old, was a small, stocky man whose bulldog physique and jutting jaw bespoke his sheer determi-

Contributors to the SA flying club received pins such as this one, which displays a glider and the motto, "Sport flying helps Germany."

nation. He had met Göring while serving as an aerial observer and staff officer in World War I. The two were never close friends but frequently helped each other along. After Göring entered the Reichstag as a Nazi representative in 1928, he received handsome "consulting fees" from Milch to promote Lufthansa's interests. Three years later Göring introduced Milch to Hitler, and the politically astute Milch made Lufthansa aircraft available to the Nazi leader, who flew 23,000 miles on speechmaking tours during the frenzied political campaigns of 1932. The contribution to the eventual Nazi triumph was considerable, and not merely logistical; the familiar sight of Hitler stepping from a sleek aircraft gave him the appearance of a man of the future.

When Milch learned that he was being considered for the second spot at the Air Ministry, he ruthlessly removed what could have been a fatal impediment; he made his mother sign and publish a sworn statement that he had been fathered not by her husband, who was a Jew, but by a German aristocrat during a previously undisclosed, adulterous relationship. Milch became known among cynics as the "honorary Aryan."

With uncompromising brusqueness, Milch waded into the awesome problems facing the aircraft industry. In two and a half days of nonstop work, he and his aides planned in detail how to build the thousand-airplane fleet recommended by Felmy. Milch's expectations jolted the manufacturers as if with a cattle prod. During an early inspection he asked officials of the Junkers firm how many Ju 52s—trimotor transports that were easily converted to bombers—they could assemble in a year. They said eighteen, if all other projects were dropped from production. He gave them twelve months to produce 178 Ju 52s, plus 45 trainers. Heinkel managers were similarly startled when Milch's aide, Colonel Albert Kesselring, ordered them to begin work at once on a new plant at Rostock that would employ 3,000 workers, or nearly as many as the entire industry had employed when Hitler took power.

The Air Ministry resorted to various schemes to subsidize this urgent buildup of air power. Some companies received outright grants or were taken over by the government, as in the case of the struggling Junkers. Other firms were given covert support so that the scope of the buildup could be concealed from the Allies. Low-interest and interest-free loans were channeled to manufacturers through a dummy corporation set up by the Air Ministry. And by 1934 Schacht's Mefo bills—privately issued certificates that were in fact backed by the government—were paying for much of the air industry's expansion.

At first, the industry produced those models that had been developed with the Versailles strictures in mind—unarmed trainers, He 45 and He 46

Downfall of a Pacifist Plane Maker

White-haired Hugo Junkers (*center*) congratulates two pilots in 1927 after a record fifty-two-hour flight in a Junkers W-33.

One prominent victim of Hermann Göring's campaign to reorganize German aviation was Hugo Junkers, the elderly aircraft designer and builder whose creations had won plaudits and prizes around the world. To the leaders of the new Nazi order, Junkers was suspect both for his avowed commitment to democracy and for his pacifist leanings. Although financial constraints had compelled Junkers to abet the Reichswehr in the 1920s by producing military aircraft in Russia, he fervently hoped that the airplane would become "a weapon of happy humanitarianism" and deplored Germany's rush to rearm.

In the spring of 1933, Göring and Erhard Milch, a one-time Junkers executive, pressured Junkers to sever his ties to the firm that bore his name. Junkers resisted, but his opponents threatened to open an official inquiry into two charges against him—that he had claimed expenses at his Russian plant that were incurred at his German factories, and that he had leaked details of Germany's secret rearmament to socialists in the Reichstag. Shaken, Junkers sold a controlling interest in the company to the government. But Göring and Milch were not content. They held the seventy-five-year-old industrialist under house arrest in Bavaria for several months until he promised to divest himself of his remaining stock.

Hugo Junkers died a dejected man in February 1935. Two months later, the company he once owned was fully nationalized, the better to serve the Nazi regime in its drive for air supremacy.

The single-seat Ar 64 biplanes flying in wing-tip formation at top left were used to train fighter pilots at a secret school in southern Germany during the early 1930s. At bottom left, an SA band and color guard perform in 1933 at the christening of the *Hindenburg*, a four-engine Junkers G-38. Built as a passenger plane for Lufthansa, it could easily be converted into a military transport.

reconnaissance craft, transports such as the Ju 52 that might quickly be converted to bombers. Meanwhile, development of purely military planes, such as the Arado fighter Ar 68 and the Do 11 bomber, continued in secret, but none was yet ready for mass production.

By early 1934 Milch's strenuous efforts were yielding results. Employment in the aircraft industry reached 16,000, a fourfold increase from the year before. To speed the production of particular models, patterns for their various components were sent from a central shop to a number of factories; the finished components were then dispatched to huge assembly plants. With the help of such innovations, the industry's monthly output reached seventy-two aircraft, more than double its 1933 pace. At the same time, two million German workers were laboring to expand the nation's existing network of airfields, control towers, and supply depots, with each of the projects concealed under a false name. The new military airfield at Jüterbog, near Berlin, for example, was labeled the Air Transport Office of the Reich Autobahn, while a nearby supply depot was called the German Glider-Research Institute.

Even as Germany geared up for a full-fledged air force, a vigorous debate raged about the objective of that force. Most army officers, and even most aviators who had earned their stripes in World War I, saw the air force's mission as a tactical one. Reconnaissance aircraft should spot enemy formations for the infantry and targets for the artillery; then tactical bombers should support infantry attacks with strafing and pinpoint-bombing runs while fighters fend off enemy aircraft.

In opposition to this view, a small but determined group of visionaries espoused a new doctrine of air power, one that would require a different kind of air force. In their view, war was no longer a clash of armies but of societies, a conflict in which not only enemy formations but distant factories, centers of government, and even such intangibles as civilian morale must be seen as targets. In such a war the air force should serve not as an auxiliary to the army and navy, but as a separate arm with its own distinct strategic mission. The key components of this strategic air force would be heavy, long-range bombers capable of penetrating deep into enemy territory to destroy the enemy's capacity and will to wage war.

Among the adherents of this doctrine was Robert Knauss, commander of the Air Ministry's Training Squadron. The author of several books on aviation theory, Knauss composed a long memorandum in 1933 arguing that the swift development of a strategic bomber force would give Germany a prohibitive edge over its two chief territorial rivals, France and Poland. Even if the two countries united against Germany, he argued, the bombers would guarantee a German victory. Knauss went so far as to include a

99

detailed order of battle for such a campaign, but he also emphasized how the strategic force could prevent war by intimidating any potential foe.

The leading proponent of the strategic approach within the Air Ministry, however, was Walther Wever, Göring's chief of staff. Wever was a professional soldier with a penetrating and inventive mind. During World War I, he had helped devise the concept of elastic defense, which called for the forward positions of an infantry line to be abandoned during an artillery bombardment, then reoccupied in time to meet the ensuing infantry attack. On taking office in 1933, Wever received no guidance from Göring or Milch on what kind of war the air force should be prepared to fight. So he read *Mein Kampf*, analyzed the European political situation for himself, and concluded that Germany's primary enemy would be Soviet Russia. Defeating that giant country, he reasoned, would require a strategic air force capable of destroying the Soviets' war-making capability quickly, at its source. To this end, Wever in 1934 gave top priority to the design and development of a heavy four-engine bomber that would be capable of flying 2,000 miles into Russia.

As it happened, misfortune awaited both the chief of staff and his cherished project: It would take two problem-plagued years to produce the first

Atop an aluminum-alloy wing, 100 workers demonstrate the strength of a new flying boat at the Rohrbach factory near Berlin. The single cantilever wing and sweeping lines were trademarks of the plane's designer, Adolf Rohrbach.

Visitors to the Institute for Experimental Flight in Adlershof, a Berlin suburb, pass beneath a propeller twenty-six feet in diameter. Driven by a 2,700-horsepower engine, the prop was part of a wind tunnel where new aircraft were tested.

heavy-bomber prototype, and soon after it came off the line—with badly flawed engines—Wever died in the crash of his own plane. But well before that, while the heavy bomber was still a concept on the drawing board, army generals were making a powerful case against the entire strategic approach. They found it difficult to focus on the seemingly remote threat posed by the Soviets when Germany was not yet fully equipped to defend its own borders. And as for Knauss's argument that a strategic force would give Germany the upper hand over France and Poland, the generals countered that tactical aircraft had sufficient range to hit most of the vital targets in both countries, albeit to less devastating effect.

The critics realized, too, that making an all-out commitment to the development of heavy bombers would deprive the army of the swarms of fighters and tactical bombers on which the generals would rely. By late 1934 both Göring and Hitler were convinced that the army would have to be placated, although neither man was willing to surrender the strategic option altogether. The result was a compromise. Work on strategic bombers would continue on a scaled-down level, while production of tactical aircraft would be pushed ahead.

By the time Hitler publicly proclaimed the existence of the German air force in the spring of 1935, the emphasis had shifted to the development of a plane that could play either a tactical or a limited strategic role—a medium bomber with a range of up to 1,000 miles, a payload of up to 2,200 pounds, and a speed of at least 200 miles per hour.

Since no existing prototype satisfied all the criteria, the air force, or Luftwaffe, chose to develop three. One bomber, the Ju 86, was hampered by design problems and would never play an important part in the Luftwaffe's scheme. A second, the Do 17, was an adaptation of a high-speed passenger plane designed for Lufthansa. To achieve its intended speed of more than 200 miles per hour, the designers had to make the passenger cabin so small that it could carry just six cramped travelers. Luft-

hansa rejected the design, and the Luftwaffe inherited it—the product of a compromise, the plane could outrun any fighter in the sky but could carry only one 550-pound bomb.

The third medium bomber—the He 111—was also tailored for a civilian role, but its designers at least had military applications in mind. As employed by the airline Lufthansa, the He 111 carried ten passengers in two cabins. Between them was an unusually large space dubbed the smoking compartment. In its military guise, the smoking section became the bay for four 550-pound bombs.

All the medium bombers in the Luftwaffe's arsenal shared a flaw—a tricky bombsight that could be mastered only through extensive practice. More often than not, pilots on training runs missed their targets. In time, a better bombsight would be designed. But in the interim, concern for accuracy led the Luftwaffe to stress the development of a first-class dive bomber, a warplane whose limited load but pinpoint delivery would suit it perfectly for the destruction of vital tactical targets such as bridges, ships, and artillery emplacements. The Germans called this type of aircraft a *Sturzkampfflugzeug*, or diving attack plane, a term that was soon shortened to the evocative *Stuka*.

The man who championed the Stuka was another veteran of the vaunted Flying Circus squadron, Ernst Udet. During World War I Udet was credited with downing a phenomenal sixty-two enemy planes, and he was understandably miffed when Göring was chosen over him to command the squadron in 1918. But the undercurrent of rivalry between the two was offset by their mutual determination to restore German mastery of the air. By early 1936 Udet was head of the Luftwaffe's Technical Office, where he played a decisive role in evaluating the various Stuka prototypes designed by competing German firms and selecting the one that would enter production. Always eager to take to the air, Udet personally tested one of the leading contenders, the He 118. Somehow the flight went awry, and Udet was forced to bail out over a cornfield. Rescuers found him tangled in his parachute, bruised but unbroken, muttering about that "damn death

Resplendent in a white uniform, deputy Luftwaffe chief Erhard Milch confers with designer Willy Messerschmitt beneath the streamlined spinner of an early model of Messerschmitt's swift, all-metal fighter, the Bf 109.

trap." Udet's mood improved the next day when the plane's designer, Ernst Heinkel, visited him in the hospital with six splits of champagne, which the two polished off in an hour.

The crash failed to deter Udet from trying out another dive bomber, the Ju 87. The plane, with its wings distinctively slanted upward like those of a gull in flight, could dive at a much steeper angle than the He 118, and it performed flawlessly in Udet's hands. Before the year was out, the Ju 87 entered a long production cycle that would ultimately make the word *Stuka* a dreaded one on many fronts.

Others in the Luftwaffe, meanwhile, had been looking critically at Germany's small battery of fighter prototypes—an arsenal that in 1933 consisted entirely of biplanes such as the Ar 68 and the He 51. Both were serviceable models, but they would soon be outdated. The problem lay in their very configuration. As planes flew faster—surpassing 200 miles per hour—drag, or the resistance to foward motion created by the aircraft's surface area, became more pronounced. Inevitably, the two tiers of a biplane created more drag than a single-wing craft. Thus the production of a monoplane fighter was essential if Germany hoped to achieve air supremacy. By late 1935 a competition was under way to produce such a fighter, and it proved every bit as intense as the contest to build the Stuka.

This time the advantage lay with the firm of Willy Messerschmitt, a prickly, painstaking designer who had a genius for both the theoretical and the practical sides of aircraft construction. Messerschmitt's Bf 109—so called for the Bayrische Flugzeugwerke, or Bavarian Aircraft Works, that produced the prototype—was a marvelously sleek, all-metal creation that reached test speeds of nearly 300 miles per hour. Impressive though it was, that performance was nearly matched by the entry of the tenacious Heinkel—the He 112; and the Heinkel monoplane proved easier to handle on the runway than the Bf 109, with its narrowly spaced landing gear. In the end, Messerschmitt's attention to the assembly line made the difference. He had evolved a system of mass production at his works that enabled him to turn out fighters faster and more economically than Heinkel, and late in 1936 he won the contract. Over the next two years, Messerschmitt would produce more than 700 Me 109s—as the plane became known—a feat that gave Germany a tactical edge as war loomed in Europe.

While Göring's Luftwaffe was taking wing, Guderian pressed on with his campaign to mechanize the army. The unpopularity of his proposals among some influential generals in no way deterred him, for he had been bred to defend his convictions no less forcefully than he would his country.

Like his father before him, Guderian was a Prussian officer. Membership

in that caste required not only the highly developed sense of punctilious-ness for which it was often ridiculed, but adherence to a tradition of tough-minded debate. Prussian officers were indeed expected to render absolute obedience to a superior—but only after giving him the benefit of their most critical thinking and vigorous argument. Guderian was popular with his subordinates for affording their ideas lengthy and unfailingly polite consideration. But not all of Guderian's superior officers appreciated it when Guderian asked the same of them.

He had begun criticizing the system when he was just twenty-four years of age, in the spring of 1913. After serving for five years with his father's unit, the young officer had been given a choice of technical training in either machine guns or signals. On his father's advice—that machine guns had "no future" in warfare and that wireless radio was an up-and-coming field—Guderian chose signals. And after participating in one of the army's first exercises involving the bulky and unreliable radios of the day, Guderian wrote an indignant report. No one had determined the proper uses of the equipment, he complained, and his detachment had frequently been left on its own, without orders, unable to contribute anything. Guderian said later that the complaint went to his commanding general and "disappeared into his desk."

The shortcomings Guderian had identified were still much in evidence when war broke out more than a year later. The radio equipment of the era had severe shortcomings; the cumbersome, battery-powered sets were fragile, easily jammed by conflicting signals, and impossible to tune as they jounced along on horse-drawn wagons. As for its function, the radio was being used as just another tool for relaying the generals' orders down the line. Nevertheless, Guderian saw enormous possibilities if the sets were improved and used to keep generals in touch with events along the battle fronts and in close communication with their line commanders.

Beyond the matter of communications, Guderian perceived that the traditional ways of making war were fast becoming obsolete. He saw the cavalry made ineffective in combat by modern infantry weapons and in reconnaissance by aircraft, and the horse supplanted as a means of transport by motor vehicles. He saw warfare frozen into entrenched immobility by the butchery of automatic weapons. He witnessed the tragic inefficiency of prolonged artillery barrages and massed infantry attacks. Again and again he was outraged by the failure of the generals to understand the obsolescence and initiate change.

As fate would have it, Guderian did not witness the first effective use of the tactic that was to alter warfare—and his own career—forever. He was not at Cambrai in November 1917 when the British, forsaking the estab-

Heinz Guderian *(far right)* escorts Defense Minister Otto Gessler *(center)* and Gessler's adjutant during maneuvers at Mecklenburg in 1925. When Guderian proposed that motorized units be upgraded from supply to combat duty, his commander responded: "To hell with combat! They're supposed to carry flour!"

lished practice of using tanks piecemeal to support the infantry, attacked with massed armor and achieved a precedent-setting breakthrough. Three months later, as a new member of the German General Staff Corps, Guderian studied gloomy reports as the kaiser's beleaguered army, which had less than two dozen tanks of its own, struggled vainly to repulse the Allied armored thrusts that helped end the war.

For Guderian, the signing of the armistice and the fall of the monarchy were occasions for sorrow and recrimination. "Our beautiful German empire is no more," he wrote to his wife from Munich on November 14, 1918, as leftists took to the streets to celebrate the kaiser's downfall. "Villains have torn everything to the ground. All comprehension of justice and order, duty and decency, seems to have been destroyed. I only regret not having civilian clothing here in order not to expose to the jostling mob the clothes that I have worn with honor for twelve years." Guderian, however, remained in the army, and in 1922 he was given a critical assignment in the Inspectorate of Transport Troops—to study the use of motorized units in the forward-looking Reichswehr that General Hans von Seeckt was nurturing.

In characteristic fashion, Guderian looked beyond the practical aspects of his assignment to its broad implications for the theory of warfare. Pondering the lessons he had learned in World War I and studying the conclusions of military analysts in Germany and other European countries, he evolved a concept he called *Stosskraft*, or decisive force. This he defined as "the force that allows the soldier in combat to bring his weapons close enough to the enemy to destroy him." Massed infantry, firing volleys before pressing the attack with bayonets, once had decisive force, he said, but had been neutralized by the machine gun. Artillery had contributed to decisive force in the last war, he added, but the big guns had generally been placed too far from their targets to hit them with sufficient accuracy. The challenge now was to concentrate the devastating firepower modern armies pos-

Colonel Guderian (*right*), chief of the Wehrmacht's new motor-transport command, confers with a subordinate during field exercises in 1935. Guderian argued that tanks not be scattered in support of the infantry but concentrated in armored divisions.

Motorcycle-platoon members *(foreground)* set up a machine gun during a 1934 demonstration that aroused Hitler's interest in mechanized warfare. On that occasion, Guderian *(at Hitler's left)* also showed the Führer the army's first armored cars, anti-tank guns, and Panzer I tanks.

sessed and move it near enough to the enemy to unleash its full force. With a touch of irony, Guderian noted that the answer to this contemporary problem was to be found in "the restoration of an ancient means—armor." Called *Panzer* by the Germans, armor had long since gone out of favor because neither man nor animal could carry enough to defend against modern weapons. But a motor vehicle could, Guderian declared. "Of all land forces, the tank possesses the most *Stosskraft.*"

Guderian's cogent arguments won a sympathetic hearing from high-ranking officers on the general staff, and in 1928 he was put in charge of a new tactical wing to develop the army's policy on tanks. Ever alert to outside developments, he analyzed books by such foreign theoreticians as Britain's General J. F. C. Fuller and the French colonel Charles de Gaulle. Guderian had ideas of his own, but before attempting to implement them he went through a necessary formality: He traveled to Sweden to operate a tank for the first time and to observe exercises using tanks. Buoyed by the experiences, he returned to Germany to campaign for a plan of action that stressed armored assaults to a degree neither German commanders nor their counterparts in other European countries were contemplating. It would have been heresy enough had Guderian claimed that tanks should operate independently of the other arms, but he contended that the other arms should be made subordinate to the tanks. He was convinced, he said, that in "a formation of all arms, the tanks must play the primary role."

In exercises in the summer of 1929 he demonstrated the operation of the ultimate in *Stosskraft*, the armored division. To most of the participants, the affair was high comedy. The mere idea of administrative troops—drivers and technicians—leading an attack was enough to set an experienced infantryman laughing. But there was more humor involved. Since Germany's covert program to produce a serviceable tank had yet to yield results, the attack was carried out by little automobiles draped with canvas and sheet iron to resemble tanks. The vehicles looked ridiculous, carried no weapons, and could not cross the most trifling of obstacles. At every opportunity, the contemptuous foot soldiers in the exercise punched holes in the tanks' flimsy "armor" with their bayonets.

Nevertheless, so fervent was Guderian in explaining and interpreting the methods being tried that he was encouraged to continue his experiments. "The idea gained ground," he recalled, "that it was essential to have a panzer command." Yet Guderian still faced strong opposition. Senior infantry officers, long accustomed to having the other arms of the service subordinate to them, could not see the need to relinquish their standing. Some younger cavalry officers viewed tanks as an enticing alternative, but their superiors, fighting desperately to justify the cavalry after its poor showing in the last war, saw the armored command as a direct threat. The infighting was fierce.

Beyond such professional jealousy lay the suspicion in some quarters that Guderian's vision was a utopian dream that ignored economic and political realities. Such a charge was leveled bluntly by Guderian's commanding officer, the inspector of motorized troops, General Otto von Stülpnagel, who told him to his face: "You're too impetuous. Believe me, neither of us will ever see German tanks in operation during our lifetime." The evidence appeared to be on Stülpnagel's side. Since the early 1920s, the German firm of Rheinmetall had been struggling to develop a tank that could compete with those of Germany's potential enemies. The vehicle was officially referred to as a farm tractor to deceive the Interallied Military Control Commission. By 1926 Rheinmetall had put together a twenty-ton behemoth that carried a huge 75-mm gun, and shortly afterward the firm completed a lighter, nine-ton model, armed with a 37-mm gun. But both tanks were prohibitively expensive. And because no one had decided how to put the tanks to use, and hence what kind of tanks were needed, tank development was halted.

Conditions changed in the spring of 1931. The hidebound Stülpnagel was succeeded by Major General Oswald von Lutz, a former commander and old friend of Guderian and a man alive to the possibilities of the new technology. Lutz promoted Guderian to chief of staff of the Inspectorate of Motorized Troops, and the two began a fruitful partnership. Together they beat back the opposition of the cavalry and the old-line infantry, refined their tactics, devised long-range plans that included continual exercises— and ordered the first tank prototype that could realistically enter production. It appeared in 1932, a light, five-ton, two-man tank armed only with two machine guns. It was hardly the battle wagon that Guderian preferred; still, it was a tank where none had been before.

There remained a long way to go. When Hitler took power in early 1933 and set the country on the road to vigorous rearmament, his closest confidant, Hermann Göring, saw to it that aircraft were given primary consideration for funding. Undeterred, Guderian mustered what equipment he could and refined his panzer-assault concept on the training ground. His big break came early in 1934 at Kunersdorf, when he was able to demonstrate his approach to the Führer.

Although the demonstration was crude, it effectively simulated Guderian's vision for the role of armor. As Guderian pictured it, the typical panzer thrust would be led by reconnaissance troops on motorcycles or in armored cars, probing for weak spots in the enemy line and reporting by radio to a command post that would coordinate the entire assault. Then the tanks would roll up for the breakthrough. Once they penetrated the enemy line, they were not to consolidate their position or secure their line of retreat; they were simply to keep going, plunging deep into enemy territory to strike at command, communication, and supply centers. Antitank guns would be towed behind the tanks to help cope with enemy armor and to defend captured positions, and infantry would follow in trucks or tractors to secure the flanks as the tanks forged ahead. Instead

Turning "Tractors" into Tanks

Well before the strictures that were imposed at Versailles were publicly disavowed, Weimar Germany was secretly developing its first experimental tanks and calling them "agricultural tractors." In December of 1933 the government contracted Krupp to build the *Panzerkampfwagen*, or armored battle wagon, that is shown below. Adapted from a British design and no bigger than a motorcar, the Panzer I was underarmed and underarmored. But it was a start, and Hitler's forces eventually had 1,800 of them.

Better vehicles already were in the pipeline. The Panzer IIc *(top right)*, introduced in 1935, had armor almost twice as thick as the original and carried a small cannon in its revolving turret. The first in a series of *Panzerspähwagen*, or armored scout cars *(bottom right)*, was introduced in 1937 and initially carried only machine guns; the early models could reach forty-eight miles per hour on the open road.

Panzer IA

The so-called Father of the Panzers carried two light machine guns and could achieve a speed of twenty-three miles per hour. The tank's half-inch-thick armor, however, made it vulnerable to anything heavier than small-arms fire.

Panzer IIc

At ten tons, the Panzer IIc weighed nearly twice as much as its predecessor and accommodated a crew of three instead of two. The 20-mm cannon and 7.92-mm machine gun in its turret made the IIc competitive with enemy light tanks.

Panzerspähwagen 221

This armored scout car was equipped with a single machine gun mounted in a flat, open-topped turret. Four-wheel drive and steering gave the scout car maneuverability and a satisfactory cross-country performance.

of a long, brutal hammering along the enemy's front, this would be a sharp, surgical strike at the foe's central nervous system, designed to paralyze.

When Hitler exclaimed "That's what I need!" Guderian's star began to rise. In June a panzer command was officially organized, with General Lutz as its chief and Guderian as its chief of staff. By 1935 panzer commanders down to the company level were equipped with rugged and reliable radios. And Guderian and Lutz were specifying new kinds of tanks to replace the inadequate Panzer I. These were the Panzer II, an upgraded version of its predecessor, with a 20-mm main gun and slightly thicker armor; the Panzer III, designed to be a tank killer with a 37-mm gun; and the Panzer IV, a versatile tank with a 75-mm gun and a 125-mile range for deep penetration into enemy areas. None of these models would be available for a few years. And the limited funds available made them compromises. The armor of Panzers I and II was too thin to withstand anything but small-arms fire. And while the Panzers III and IV would have thicker skins, both France and England were developing tanks that were more heavily armored.

Determined to strengthen Germany's "will to arms," Hitler decrees the renewal of military conscription before a somber Reichstag on March 16, 1935.

On parade at Potsdam, the residence of emperors and bedrock of Prussian militarism, a new regiment salutes War Minister Blomberg. The drafting of twenty-one-year-olds—begun in 1935—increased Germany's armed forces to 300,000 men.

Beneath the surface limitations of these early panzers, however, lay a basic strength—the first-rate design of their engines, transmissions, and tracks. This made them dependable under grueling combat conditions and eased the task of producing more powerful models in the future; designers could add thicker armor and larger guns to the formula and be assured that the mechanical workings would bear the strain. Moreover, the heavy tanks that Germany's rivals were turning out had serious problems. The French Char-B that appeared in the late 1930s, for example, boasted armor four times as thick as that of the Panzer IV, but the Char-B's big 75-mm gun was fixed in place; the turret of its counterpart, the Panzer IV, swiveled. Such design flaws, coupled with the failure of French tacticians to understand that the future effectiveness of tanks depended more on speed and co-ordination than on sheer weight or firepower, would have devastating consequences for the French when German panzer corps rolled across their border in the spring of 1940.

Fittingly, one of those corps would be led by Guderian, whose career as a field commander was launched in October of 1935, when he was trans-ferred from his staff position to take charge of one of three fledgling panzer divisions. As Guderian set out that autumn to school his vanguard in a new mode of warfare, thousands of other German officers were caught up in a more prosaic duty—the task of turning civilians into soldiers for the ex-panded army that Hitler had called for publicly in March. Ironically, Hitler's stated goal—a force of thirty-six 10,000-man divisions—was precisely the

sort of buildup that the top generals had been advocating for a while. But whereas they had envisioned reaching the target some time in 1938 or 1939, Hitler now wanted it done by the beginning of 1936. Meeting the deadline left commanders little room for novel approaches. Tens of thousands of fresh recruits would need basic training, and plenty of it.

The sudden expansion taxed the army's small officer corps. The army had already been compelled to shorten the training period for officer candidates. Now a number of retired officers were brought back to fill administrative and technical posts, and officers from the SA and the Landespolizei, the militarized state police, were absorbed by the thousands. Many of the new arrivals were far removed from the aristocratic traditions of the old Reichswehr, a situation that helped breed a closer relationship between officers and enlisted men in Hitler's new Wehrmacht.

The army's chief asset as it hustled to train the new recruits, however, was a ready supply of superbly schooled noncommissioned officers. In the select 100,000-man force that General Seeckt had nurtured, privates were fully as proficient as sergeants and corporals in the armies of rival nations. As the army expanded, those polished privates were more than ready to step up to the NCO level and work the recruits into shape. In time, they would help mold one of the best-trained armies in the world.

But the initial effect of the expansion was the breakup of the old, elite force. The battalions of an existing regiment were detached to form the

Germany's four ranking military officers—from left, War Minister Blomberg, army commander in chief Fritsch, air force chief Göring, and the navy's senior admiral, Erich Raeder—review passing troops in Berlin.

114

nucleus of two or more new regiments. It was a painstaking procedure that fell far short of meeting Hitler's timetable. By early 1936, when he drew up plans for the Rhineland occupation, the number of combat-ready regiments was hardly sufficient to match the armed strength of neighboring France. And the special panzer units that were being drilled by Guderian and his colleagues were still woefully underequipped, as German factories struggled to keep up with the demand for armored vehicles.

If Hitler had little reason to feel secure in the strength of his army or air force in the event of war, he could hope for even less from the navy, which had suffered most from the Versailles restrictions. Yet in that service, as in the others, plans were afoot for renewal. The most significant changes had been generated by the ideas of a former submarine commander who had learned some hard lessons in the Great War.

World War I ended for Lieutenant Karl Dönitz two months before the armistice in a way that would have a significant impact on World War II. In September of 1918 Dönitz, recently given command of his own submarine, arranged with another U-boat commander to attack a British convoy near Malta after it emerged from the Suez Canal on its way west. Dönitz's plan was irregular; the standard operating procedure was for U-boats to disperse, search for enemy convoys on their own, and attack alone.

In the event, the other submarine had mechanical problems and could not participate in the attack. Dönitz's U-boat was thus unaccompanied as usual when he slipped between the escorting destroyers and approached the procession of merchant vessels. He was running on the surface, depending on darkness to conceal the scant profile of his boat, and was still unseen when he launched a torpedo at point-blank range. The targeted merchantman exploded and began to sink as Dönitz took his submarine down in an emergency dive to avoid an oncoming destroyer. Soon other destroyers converged on his location. He and his men tensed for the depth charges, but none came; the submarine was too close to the convoy to be attacked without endangering the merchant ships. In the confusion, Dönitz slipped safely away.

It had been a successful foray, and Dönitz decided to try again. Shortly after dawn, submerged, he approached the convoy once more and prepared to launch a torpedo. Suddenly, his submarine tipped and began to plunge straight down into the depths. The boat had a flaw in its design: a lack of longitudinal stability that the builders had tried to correct with only incomplete success.

Desperately, Dönitz ordered the water blown from the boat's ballast tanks with compressed air to give the craft maximum buoyancy. In addi-

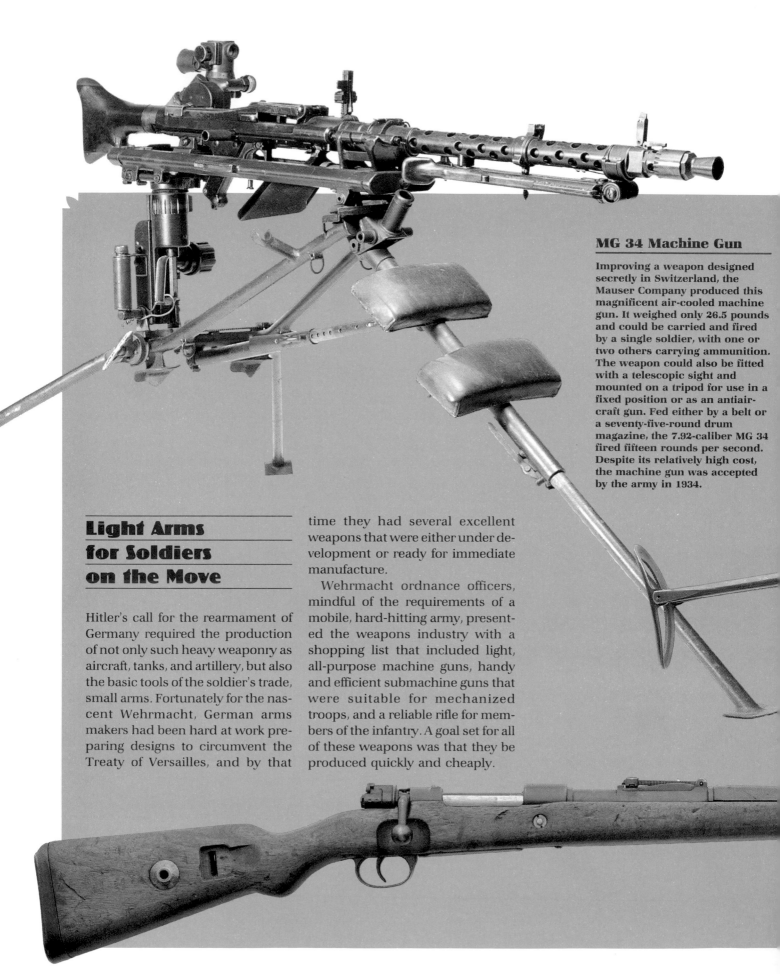

MG 34 Machine Gun

Improving a weapon designed secretly in Switzerland, the Mauser Company produced this magnificent air-cooled machine gun. It weighed only 26.5 pounds and could be carried and fired by a single soldier, with one or two others carrying ammunition. The weapon could also be fitted with a telescopic sight and mounted on a tripod for use in a fixed position or as an antiaircraft gun. Fed either by a belt or a seventy-five-round drum magazine, the 7.92-caliber MG 34 fired fifteen rounds per second. Despite its relatively high cost, the machine gun was accepted by the army in 1934.

Light Arms for Soldiers on the Move

Hitler's call for the rearmament of Germany required the production of not only such heavy weaponry as aircraft, tanks, and artillery, but also the basic tools of the soldier's trade, small arms. Fortunately for the nascent Wehrmacht, German arms makers had been hard at work preparing designs to circumvent the Treaty of Versailles, and by that time they had several excellent weapons that were either under development or ready for immediate manufacture.

Wehrmacht ordnance officers, mindful of the requirements of a mobile, hard-hitting army, presented the weapons industry with a shopping list that included light, all-purpose machine guns, handy and efficient submachine guns that were suitable for mechanized troops, and a reliable rifle for members of the infantry. A goal set for all of these weapons was that they be produced quickly and cheaply.

Walther HP Automatic Pistol

The Walther HP was the product of the Waffenfabrik Walther. Chosen to replace the reliable but expensive P 08 Luger, the HP required less costly machine work and hand-fitting. Among its innovative features was a double-action trigger that allowed the weapon to be carried safely with a round in the chamber. Issued to the Wehrmacht as the P 38, it fired the army's standard 9-mm Para-Bellum cartridge.

MP 38 Submachine Gun

Intended in 1938 for issue to crews of armored vehicles, the 9-mm MP 38 submachine gun soon became general issue to infantry platoon and section commanders. Its telescoping bolt produced a 500-round-per-minute rate of fire. The Erma Company's design, with a plastic stock, stamped sheet-metal and die-cast parts, and a breech block that needed a minimum of machine work, was streamlined for mass production. The submachine gun also incorporated a folding metal butt.

Carbine 98k

The Mauser rifle was the Wehrmacht's basic infantry weapon. In the 1920s Reichswehr ordnance experts had shortened the 1898 carbine. Renamed Carbine 98k, it was issued in 1935. Handier and lighter than its World War I forerunner, it retained the Mauser's robust bolt action and fired a 7.92-mm cartridge from a five-round, clip-loaded, box magazine. A reinforced hole in the butt allowed the weapon to be locked in storage racks.

tion, he ordered the engine run full astern in an attempt to pull the boat back from the bottom before the rapidly increasing pressure cracked the hull. At last the descent stopped, a full hundred feet below the boat's maximum rated depth. Then the craft lurched toward the surface. "Like a stick plunged under water and then suddenly released," Dönitz recalled, "it shot upward and out of the water to arrive with a crash on the surface. I tore open the conning-tower hatch and glanced hastily all around. It was now broad daylight. I found that we were right in the middle of the convoy. All the ships, destroyers and merchantmen alike, were flying signal flags, sirens were howling all around us." Within minutes, the U-boat was surrounded by destroyers, riddled with shell holes, and sinking. Dönitz gave the order to abandon ship.

Dönitz spent the next nine months in a British prisoner-of-war camp, pondering the lessons of his last raid and of submarine warfare in general. What worried him was not the mechanical failure that had doomed his U-boat; that was a matter for engineers. As a commander, Dönitz was

Initiated in secret, the first four U-boats of Germany's new underseas fleet are commissioned at Kiel in 1935. These type-IIA boats displaced only 250 tons and were so unstable when running on the surface that their crews called them "dugout canoes."

Karl Dönitz, the future flag officer of Germany's submarine fleet, stands watch on the conning tower of U-39 during a combat patrol in World War I.

concerned with a tactical problem—the long odds faced by a single U-boat attacking a well-guarded convoy. The Allies had developed the convoy system in midwar to deal with the U-boat threat, and in Dönitz's opinion German submarine tactics had proven unequal to the challenge: U-boats continued to prowl the sea lanes alone, or on rare occasions, in pairs.

As Dönitz well knew, a U-boat encountered a convoy mostly by accident. Radio communications were infrequent and unreliable, and a submarine's speed was slow and its range limited. Under these conditions, a U-boat's preferred tactic was to take up a station somewhere in a sea lane and wait until a convoy happened by. If it did, the submarine attacked and fought for as long as it could. "The lone U-boat might well sink one or two of the ships, or even several," Dönitz noted, "but that was but a poor percentage of the whole." The answer, Dönitz concluded, was to attack as wolves—in a pack. "Against the massed ships of a convoy," he reasoned, "the only right course is to engage with every available U-boat simultaneously."

Just how to manage that, given the poor methods of reconnaissance and communication available at the time, was a question Dönitz puzzled over during his captivity and hoped to think out when he returned home. Repatriated in July of 1919, he agreed to stay on in Germany's tiny postwar navy only when assured that Germany would someday replace the U-boat fleet it had surrendered to the Allies.

But Dönitz would have to wait far longer than he realized at the time. The German navy, in fact, was more stringently controlled by the commissioners of the Versailles treaty than any other service. The surface fleet was reduced to thirty-six ships—six battleships, six cruisers, twelve destroyers, and twelve torpedo boats—and the building of additional ships was banned. Even if the navy had managed to persuade the German government to defy the treaty and provide secret funding for new warships or U-boats, the large construction projects involved in shipbuilding would have been virtually impossible to hide from Allied inspectors.

Before Hitler's rise to power, however, the navy did score one major coup in its effort to strengthen its surface fleet. In 1922, under the terms of the Washington Naval Treaty, the United States, Great Britain, Italy, France, and Japan agreed to limit their battleships to a displacement weight of 35,000 tons and their cruisers to 8,000 tons. Germany, which was allowed to replace its obsolete battleships in 1925,

had to limit such vessels to the relatively paltry weight of 10,000 tons. German designers made the best of the situation, coming up with the so-called pocket battleship. The *Deutschland* was the first ship to be produced. Launched in May 1931, it carried six 11.14-inch guns, weapons powerful enough to destroy any cruiser

from well beyond the range of the enemy's guns. And the *Deutschland* was fast enough to elude larger, more heavily armed enemy battleships.

Meanwhile, Krupp engineers were drawing up blueprints and supervising submarine construction for foreign countries through IVS, the firm's holding company in the Netherlands. This furtive program not only kept German designers at the forefront of submarine development but provided German commanders and crews with opportunities to take the vessels on lengthy trial runs before they were delivered to their purchasers. In return for services rendered, Krupp was able to obtain diesel engines, periscopes, and other critical U-boat parts from foreign shipbuilders. Those parts were stockpiled at Kiel, Germany's main navy yard, to await the day when the restraints of Versailles were cast off.

Germany's hopes for naval rearmament received a boost in 1934, when Hitler decided to build submarines in secret. As it happened, the need for secrecy was soon eliminated. In June of that year, just three months after unilaterally repudiating the Versailles treaty, Hitler pulled off something even more remarkable: a treaty with Britain that redefined the size of the German navy in terms distinctly favorable to the Reich. To emphasize his desire to remain on friendly terms with Britain, Hitler offered to hold the size of Germany's navy to 35 percent that of the British fleet, with the German U-boat component limited to 45 percent of the British submarine force. Britain, preoccupied at the time with a naval threat posed by Japan, happily agreed, thinking that it was merely ensuring future peace by restraining Hitler's expansionist schemes. In fact, the treaty formula was anything but a limitation on Germany's tiny navy; it represented a target that could be met only by furious shipbuilding.

Now that it had a license to expand, the German navy faced some difficult choices. Construction commenced on a pair of aircraft carriers, but neither would become operational; the naval aviation program was largely assimilated by Göring's air force. The building of new heavy battleships and

Pennants whipping in the breeze, the *Admiral Graf Spee* (right) slides down the ways in the North Sea port of Wilhelmshaven on June 30, 1935. A so-called pocket battleship, the *Graf Spee* (shown in profile above) boasted six eleven-inch guns and a top speed of twenty-eight knots.

cruisers, meanwhile, was delayed by a debate over what type of power plant to equip them with. Only in the case of submarines did the naval buildup yield immediate results. As a result of Hitler's decision in 1934 to proceed with U-boat construction, the first new submarine was launched at Kiel two days before the signing of the Anglo-German Naval Agreement. By year's end, there were fourteen submarines in the German fleet, most of them small, 250-ton types.

The training of crews could now begin in earnest. To supervise the task, Admiral Erich Raeder looked to the man who had been waiting sixteen years for just such an opportunity, Karl Dönitz. Since the war, Dönitz had commanded a destroyer, a flotilla of destroyers, and then a cruiser, acquiring what he called "the requisite complement to my war experience in U-boats." Now he returned to his old calling with undiminished enthusiasm. "Body and soul," he wrote later, "I was once more a submariner."

Although Dönitz was delighted with the spirit and determination of his trainees, there was much that needed to be done before they could fulfill the mission he envisioned for them. He assumed that in any large-scale war Germany's enemies would use the convoys that had worked so well in World War I. And so, like Guderian with his tanks, Dönitz wanted his U-boats equipped with the latest in radio equipment to coordinate group assaults. Once such equipment was in place, he planned to go a step further and assign a command submarine to lead each of the groups—or wolf packs, as they came to be known. And to eliminate the aimless waiting and wandering that had characterized U-boat sorties in World War I, Dönitz wanted reconnaissance aircraft in large numbers to scout for convoys and relay their findings to the wolf-pack commanders.

More than anything else, though, he wanted more U-boats. By 1936 construction of larger, 500-ton U-boats was under way, but the pace was slow, hampered by a shortage of shipyard space and raw materials. On average, the fleet was expanding at a rate of less than two submarines a month—a discouraging statistic for Dönitz, who saw Britain, with its huge merchant marine, as an inevitable foe.

In articulating these various demands, Dönitz was simply joining the chorus of anxious voices rising from every branch of the armed services. But, their concerns notwithstanding, Germany had made significant progress in rearming its navy, air corps, and army by early 1936, and it stood poised on the verge of a dramatic breakthrough. The combined factors of technological innovation and fresh tactical thinking were lending an impetus to the German military machine that none of its rivals could match. If the process were to continue unchecked, the German high command within a few years could realistically shift its emphasis from planning the

Germany's surface fleet, largely comprising small coastal-defense vessels, parades past Hitler's flagship in the Baltic Sea in May 1936. Although some new warships were coming on line, the navy remained Germany's neglected service. "I cannot conceive of a European war," said Hitler, "that will hang in the balance because of a few ships."

defense of the Reich's borders to plotting a war of aggressive conquest.

It was Germany's great military potential—evident now to all of Europe—that made Hitler's plan to remilitarize the Rhineland both fraught with risk and pregnant with potential reward. The reward Hitler sought was not just security for the industrially vital area, but the chance to score a major psychological victory over France and Britain. If, as he anticipated, those powers failed to react, he foresaw little difficulty in completing his military buildup unchallenged. But if, as War Minister Blomberg feared, the Allies opposed the Rhineland move in earnest, then all the hard-won German gains of the last sixteen years might be wiped out in a brief and bitter war. On the eve of this fateful gamble, even the normally sanguine Hermann Göring lost his nerve and worried aloud to Hitler that "the British and French will come in and squash us like flies." Given the unfinished state of German rearmament, it was a logical conclusion. But Hitler was not interested in such irresolute reasoning, and his icy reply proved to be correct. "Not," he said, "if we buzz loudly enough." ✚

Portent of the Storms Ahead

Beginning in 1934, Hitler flaunted the once-secret buildup of German arms by staging spectacular military exercises on the closing day of the annual Nazi rally at Nuremberg. The first of these Wehrmacht Days was a revelation both to foreign observers and to the German citizens who thronged to the zeppelin landing field where the show unfolded. American journalist William L. Shirer noted that it was "difficult to exaggerate the frenzy of the 300,000 German spectators when they saw their soldiers go into action, heard the thunder of the guns, and smelt the powder."

In succeeding years Wehrmacht Day grew into an even more impressive pageant as new weapons and warplanes were introduced. By 1937, when the photographs here and on the succeeding pages were taken, the event had acquired an air of urgency: German troops were now embroiled in a real fight in Spain, signaling Hitler's growing belligerence. On September 11, two days before the Wehrmacht exercises, the Führer told members of the Hitler Youth standing in the rain at Nuremberg that they must be prepared "not for sunshine alone, but for stormy days . . . for self-denial, sacrifice." By September 13 the sun was shining again, but the din of guns on the zeppelin field and the foreboding drone of engines overhead lent weight to Hitler's somber forecast.

To the discerning eye, however, there were signs on this Wehrmacht Day that Germany was not yet fully prepared for war. Machine-gun crews took to the field with obsolescent guns, and the airshow included squadrons of outmoded biplanes. But Germany's rivals had similar deficiencies and were doing far less to remedy them. Overall, the display—which involved some 50,000 troops—left foreign witnesses justifiably uneasy. "There was seen today perhaps one-twentieth of what the German peacetime establishment could produce at need," wrote the correspondent for the *New York Times.* "If it is a sample of the rest, it portrays a strength no other European nation can match."

With War Minister Blomberg, Hitler launches Wehrmacht Day in 1937 by greeting army chief Fritsch (*shaking hands*), Luftwaffe head Göring, and navy commander Raeder (*far right*).

A mechanized Luftwaffe anti-aircraft regiment equipped with Krupp vehicles (*foreground*) passes in parade at Nuremberg.

Realistic Drills with Imperfect Weapons

In a mock battle on Wehrmacht Day, attacking infantry supported by Panzer I tanks make headway against the defenders, most of whom have fallen to the ground. The Panzer I was armed only with machine guns, which proved ineffective against Soviet armor in Spain.

Troops move at double time to demonstrate the deployment of land mines. The mines were buried a few inches below ground and activated by pressure plates or tripwires.

Partially screened by fumes from
a smoke grenade, troops crawl
forward under simulated fire.

A machine-gun crew hustles into
position carrying a Maxim
of World War I vintage. By 1937
German arms makers were
turning out light machine guns
to replace these bulky weapons.

Firepower to Parry Attack from the Air

Defending against a mock air raid, 88-mm antiaircraft guns designed by Krupp fire blanks at an oncoming Luftwaffe squadron. German commanders in Spain learned that, with their barrels depressed, these high-velocity guns could also be used against tanks with devastating effect.

The crew of a 37 mm antiaircraft gun takes aim at low-flying Henschel 123 biplanes. The Luftwaffe would soon drop the old-fashioned biplane from its combat fleet, but the rapid-firing gun would see extensive service throughout the coming war.

An Ominous Skyful of Bombers

Do 17s sweep in formation over the stands at Nuremberg as part of a 450-airplane review that was likened to "huge flocks of

crows flying homeward." Designed as a transport, the Do 17 served for a time as a medium-range bomber.

FOUR

Rehearsal for Blitzkrieg

Precisely at noon on March 7, 1936, a trimly uniformed Adolf Hitler stepped to the podium of the Kroll Opera House in Berlin, where Nazi Germany's powerless Reichstag met. Quietly at first, almost hesitantly, the Führer addressed the 600 deputies before him. He spoke of innocent hope and deep betrayal—of a peace-loving German people held hostage to the world's great powers, of humiliating treaties imposed in vengeance, of the threat from Soviet communism. Then the words came stronger, pouring out in waves of rising intensity, the voice seething with emotion. "I will not have the gruesome Communist International dictatorship of hate descend upon the German people!" the Führer cried, his hands flailing. Cheering, the deputies rose to their feet.

Gesturing for calm, the Führer continued. Communism, he said, posed a new and immediate danger: The Soviet Union and France had negotiated a defense pact, and the German border with France lay unprotected. As every deputy knew, international decree forbade Germany to station armed forces in the Rhineland, the demilitarized region on its western frontier. Then Hitler delivered his blockbuster. "In the interest of the primitive rights of its people to the security of their frontier," he announced, "the German government has reestablished, as from today, the absolute and unrestricted sovereignty of the Reich in the demilitarized zone."

The deputies again leaped up, their cheers reverberating. Once more Hitler raised his hand. "Men of the German Reichstag," he commanded, "in the Reich's western provinces, German troops are at this minute marching into their future peacetime garrisons. We all unite in two sacred vows. First, we swear to yield to no force whatever in restoring the honor of our people. Second, we pledge that now, more than ever, we shall strive for an understanding between the European peoples. We have no territorial demands to make! Germany will never break the peace!"

It was an astonishing performance. To frenzied shouts of "Sieg Heil!" Hitler descended from the podium perspiring and exhausted, a thin smile of satisfaction playing on his lips. At grave risk of retaliation from the western powers, German soldiers had indeed marched into the Rhineland.

With a flower decorating one jacket pocket and a campaign medal adorning the other, a veteran of the Spanish Civil War takes part in the festivities that welcomed home Germany's Condor Legion in 1939.

133

For most Rhinelanders, the Wehrmacht's arrival was a signal for joyous celebration. In city after city, as the steel-helmeted battalions marched in the crowds surged into the streets to greet them. There was dancing and cheering and the singing of patriotic anthems. There were impromptu ceremonies in which young fräuleins handed red carnations to regimental officers. In Cologne one dignified burgher on his way to church did a smart about-face and headed for the main square. "The first soldier I get my hands on," he proclaimed, "is going to get as cockeyed-drunk at my expense as I did when I was a soldier in 1914—and I'm going to get cockeyed with him. Heil Hitler!" In Frankfurt it was the same, in Aachen, Düsseldorf, and Koblenz—an effusion of patriotic fervor.

Not all Germans were equally happy with the Rhineland coup, to be sure, and among the doubters were some of the army's highest-ranking generals. These officers knew too well that the Wehrmacht, despite its recent expansion, was far from ready to wage war against a major power. Germany in 1936 fielded at most twenty-five full-strength divisions; France could call up more than a hundred. And essential equipment was lacking. Mindful of such deficiencies, the planners of the Rhineland operation had deliberately limited the effort, hoping to fend off a hostile response by avoiding any semblance of a threat to French territory. Of the roughly 30,000 men who took part, only three battalions—perhaps 3,000 troops in all—were sent across the Rhine to the French border, and they were armed only with rifles and machine guns; no tanks or artillery moved to support them. For the same reason, the Luftwaffe committed just two of its four fighter squadrons to the operation. The restricted nature of the undertaking meant that the German forces in the Rhineland would be desperately vulnerable if the French chose to evict them. As Colonel Alfred Jodl, chief of Germany's home defense, admitted later, "Considering the position we were in, the French covering army could have blown us to pieces."

The danger of such a response had long troubled the German high command. Both France and England were sworn to defend the Locarno treaty, which confirmed the Rhineland's neutrality. And while the German generals knew that one day they would move to occupy the region, they counseled patience until their forces reached full strength. A year earlier, War Minister Werner von Blomberg had battle plans drawn up as a contingency measure, but he so feared disclosure of the order he scribbled it by hand and allowed no copies. He hoped the project would be dropped.

Then in early February of 1936, while Blomberg was in Bavaria attending the winter Olympics, Hitler called in General Werner von Fritsch, the army's commander in chief. The moment had come, he declared, to remilitarize the Rhineland. Fritsch agreed but urged that the operation be conducted

Smiling women press bouquets on Wehrmacht cavalry as they clatter through a flag-decked street on March 7, 1936, the day Hitler defied Germany's western neighbors by remilitarizing the Rhineland.

so as to reduce the risk of war with the Allies—a condition Hitler accepted in principle. Fritsch then had second thoughts about the wisdom of even a limited venture and tried to talk Hitler out of it. But the Führer's mind was made up. At the end of February, after Blomberg returned to Berlin, he was ordered to mobilize the army in a week's time and march it out.

Against his better judgment, the war minister went to work. The plan for the operation was called *Winterübung*, or Winter Exercise. The tension in the War Ministry, one staffer remembered, was like that at "a roulette table when a player stakes his fortune on a single number." At first, it appeared that the gamble of March 7 might fail. Stung by the surprise German move, France quickly sent thirteen divisions to reinforce its already-bristling Maginot line. The German embassy in London put the chance of war at fifty-fifty. Blomberg viewed the situation with increasing agitation, repeatedly calling Hitler's adjutant for reports and demanding an audience with the Führer. Supported by Fritsch, he sent a telegram to Hitler urging him to withdraw the three battalions from across the Rhine. By the time the two men met, on March 9, Blomberg had calmed down somewhat but in Hitler's opinion was still behaving like a "hysterical maiden." In truth, the Führer himself showed signs of strain. He paced the floor of his office in the Reich Chancellery, firing questions, restating orders. "The forty-eight hours after the march," he later conceded, "were the most nerve-racking of my life."

But as the days passed and the Wehrmacht soldiers settled into their

135

new garrisons, the tensions began to subside. France—beset with internal political problems, unsure of England's support in the crisis, and misled by grossly exaggerated reports of German strength—was not going to call Hitler's bluff after all. Flushed with success, Hitler resolved to step up the pace of German rearmament.

The objective of this accelerated buildup was to prepare Germany to deal with hostile forces on more than one front—a concern heightened by bitter memories of the nation's experience in World War I. The Reich's vulnerable frontiers would be fortified and the growing army bolstered even further. Construction of a series of blockhouses and other defenses began along the French and Belgian borders—a West Wall to confront the Maginot line. Similar fortifications were planned for the Polish border. The army's projected strength, set at thirty-six divisions the previous year, was now increased to forty-four divisions, for a total of nearly 800,000 men in uniform. The expanded force consisted of the three panzer divisions that Heinz Guderian and his colleagues were training and thirty-six infantry divisions, four of them motorized; the remainder would be so-called light divisions, made up of infantry units supported by armor—a formula devised by traditionalists in the army as an alternative to the panzer concept. The period of compulsory service for German men was lengthened from one year to two. In the event of an all-out war, which the generals thought might come as early as 1941, a call-up of reserve units would put the number of available trained soldiers at 3.6 million. Massive sums of capital were committed to fund the buildup.

Presented with this influx of personnel and money, the Wehrmacht generals could hardly complain. But the feast soon proved to be oddly difficult to digest—an embarrassment of riches that led to bottlenecks and inefficiencies. Fritsch, charged with implementing the army's latest expansion, grew frustrated. The Führer's new program, he said, was "rushing everything far too much and destroying every healthy development."

Fritsch faced the same problem that had plagued the Wehrmacht throughout its buildup—a shortage of trained officers. Despite efforts to promote qualified candidates from within the ranks and seek capable transfers from Germany's militarized police units, demand was outstripping supply. In the 1920s the army had maintained a comfortable ratio of one officer to every fourteen enlisted men; now there was one officer for every thirty-eight men. Just to preserve that proportion, 25,000 new officers would have to be commissioned quickly. Meanwhile, the reserves—vital to any mobilization plan—were going begging. With few qualified instructors available, reservists were receiving a paltry three months' training.

That the buildup engendered the insidious decay of old-school military values was no less troubling to Fritsch. Before 1933 army personnel had been expressly forbidden to engage in politics, but Nazi party ideology now permeated the very air of Germany. Many new recruits had inhaled great unthinking drafts of it. Some of them—including many former Storm Troopers—turned out to be interested more in fighting than in debating the fine points of nazism. But almost every unit contained a clique of party activists and watchful agents from Reinhard Heydrich's Security Service. The effect was to undermine the authority of the old-line commanders with their inherited notions of military discipline and detachment. To Fritsch, whose every instinct was shaped by such time-honored Prussian traditions, the army's new aspect could not have been more distasteful.

Obediently, reluctantly, Fritsch pursued his mandate to bolster the Wehrmacht. Cautious by nature, he showed little enthusiasm for the new mechanized forces that Hitler urged upon him. He preferred to develop and supply each unit in a frugal, systematic manner that sorely taxed the Reich leader's patience. Hitler was constantly chafing against "the homeopathic-like quantities which the Wehrmacht demanded . . . today an order for ten howitzers, tomorrow for two mortars, and so on." Nor did Fritsch think much of his civilian boss. "I wear my monocle," he once said, "so that my face remains stiff, especially when I confront that man."

Adding to Fritsch's difficulty was a persistent scarcity of weapons, vehicles, and fuel. Ironically, the shortfalls were occurring when Germany was enjoying civilian prosperity it had not known for decades. And this, in part, was the problem. The arms procurers had to compete with a newly robust civilian sector for Germany's limited stock of natural resources.

Even the most casual visitor could not fail to notice the outward signs of Nazi prosperity. Construction was booming. Handsome new autobahns knit the major cities one to another. Factory smokestacks billowed their salute to industrial progress. Total national income nearly doubled in only four years, and during the same period unemployment dropped from six million to a mere one million. But the recovering industries and workers were not always able to obtain the commodities they needed. Despite the Nazi party's oft-stated commitment to agriculture, farm yields had begun to fall, leading to bread shortages in the winter of 1935-1936 that caused widespread discontent. More damaging to rearmament was Germany's dependence on foreign producers of industrial staples such as iron ore, the essential ingredient of steel; virtually all iron ore had to be imported, most of it from Sweden, and Germany simply could not afford to purchase all that it needed. Synthetic fuel, meanwhile, was bubbling from the factories of I. G. Farben in ever-greater quantities but at five times the cost of the

natural product. Vast amounts of oil still had to be bought from Russia, the United States, and South America.

Reliance on imported raw materials hurt Germany's balance of payments. As huge purchases were made from foreign concerns, private capital grew increasingly scarce in the Reich, and accustomed sources of international credit dried up. The man assigned to cope with the crisis was Economics Minister Hjalmar Schacht, who proved to be a genius at financial manipulation. In May 1935 Schacht had been assigned the additional title of commissioner of the Reich war economy and thereafter faced the daunting task of reconciling the needs of the Wehrmacht and those of the German economy as a whole. His remarkable Mefo bills, kept hidden from published budgets, continued to finance arms factories, some of which received other forms of government assistance as well. To improve Germany's balance of payments, meanwhile, Schacht instituted a program that required any prospective importer to apply to the Ministry of Economics for a permit, enabling the government to limit imports to those commodities deemed essential. Schacht also resorted to barter, relying on coal, Germany's chief natural resource, and on manufactured goods.

For all his financial legerdemain, Schacht was a conservative in money matters. He knew that if the government spent too freely it risked a return to the terrible inflation of the previous decade. Hitler, too, was mindful of the dangers of inflation and heeded Schacht's warnings, but the restraints

Arriving in Budapest in a Ju 52, Germany's financial strategist, Hjalmar Schacht *(center)*, greets the head of Hungary's national bank. Schacht's tour of European capitals in the mid-1930s gained trade agreements that helped pay for Hitler's rearmament.

on his cherished armaments programs did not sit easily. Financial prudence was never a plank in the Nazi platform, and Schacht's efforts to stem expenditures were derided by party leaders. On one occasion, he protested the party's lavish use of foreign currency to fund its costly overseas propaganda campaigns. He might as well have been barking at the wind.

Frustrated, Schacht went to Hitler in the summer of 1936 and asked to be relieved of responsibility for currency exchange and the purchase of imports. Control in these matters should be given to Hermann Göring, he suggested. Perhaps Schacht thought the Luftwaffe chief would use his influence to curb the party's spendthrift ways. If so, he was mistaken. As Göring's economic authority increased, military expenditures rose apace. They soared from 5.5 billion reichsmarks in 1935 to nearly 10 billion in 1936—a full 15 percent of the nation's gross output in goods and services.

In September 1936 Göring received a new mandate—control of a four-year plan for war preparedness that Hitler unveiled at the annual Nazi rally in Nuremberg. In a memorandum to Göring in October, the Führer elaborated on the plan. The threat of international communism loomed larger, he said, and soon it would be Germany's task to defend Europe from it. Dependable sources of raw materials must be secured, if need be by seizing the territories that supply them. Additional lands must also be found for *Lebensraum*, living space, to feed and house a growing German population. Raw materials must be stockpiled and domestic production increased to prepare the Wehrmacht for the first phase of the struggle in four years' time.

Thus Germany embarked on a program of *Wehrwirtschaft*, or war economy, in which Göring and his party minions took increasing control of trade and production, along with many other aspects of national life. Shortly after assuming his lofty new post, Göring outlined his intentions before a large audience of industrialists and government officials. The age-old capitalist goal of maximum profit, he announced, must now take second place to military and political imperatives. "No limit on rearmament can be visualized," Göring went on, for "we live in a time when the final battle is in sight. All that is lacking is the actual shooting."

Such militant words notwithstanding, the Four-Year Plan was a blueprint for something less than total war. Preparation for a long war of attrition would require the German public to make drastic sacrifices that might well undermine support for the Nazi regime. Instead, Hitler and Göring pinned their hopes on an agenda that demanded economic discipline rather than outright deprivation. Planning for the battles ahead was based on the concept of blitzkrieg—lightning-fast strikes of maximum intensity that would destroy the enemy's capacity to resist. Any conflict initiated in this manner seemed likely to end in a matter of months, if not

Hitler leads his uniformed entourage up the steps of a massive podium during the 1936 Nazi party rally at Nuremberg. In his speech

to the huge crowd, the dictator announced a sweeping plan for rearmament and industrial mobilization.

141

weeks. Thus the full force of the German military machine could be committed at the outset, with no reason to hold back large reserves of men and equipment. Whatever was expended in one campaign could be made up in the interlude of peace that would presumably follow.

Even a lightning war would strain the Reich's present resources, however, so Göring acted vigorously. Thousands of directives poured forth from his offices. The most important concerned such essential raw materials as petroleum, rubber, and iron ore. Germany's objective in each case was to move beyond earlier efforts to reduce its reliance on foreign sources and become truly self-sufficient. It was a tall order. By one estimate, Germany would need more than a million tons of oil to wage war for three months— or roughly four times the amount I. G. Farben was producing annually. To remedy the deficiency, ten new synthetic-oil plants were planned. The government pledged to guarantee the price of the synthetic product and slapped a stiff tariff on imported oil. As it turned out, the program would never meet all the needs of Hitler's Reich. Yet a related effort spawned by I. G. Farben—the production of synthetic rubber—would surpass expectations, eventually exceeding both civilian and military requirements.

Shortfalls in steel production were another problem facing the so-called war economy, and Göring cast about for a solution. The nation had some iron deposits of its own, in Hanover and southern Germany, and although they were of substandard quality, Göring decided to mine them. He set up the state-owned Hermann Göring Ore and Foundry Company to do the work, with expert help from Krupp and other industrial firms. The German ores cost far more to extract and refine than the high-grade Swedish ores the Reich had been relying on, but this did not bother Göring. In the race for rearmament, expense was no object. "It is stupid to rack one's brains because of a few million marks," he declared.

The Four-Year Plan's grasp was by no means confined to a few sensitive industries. Indeed, vast sectors of the economy were subjected to the Nazi version of socialization. A pooling of patent rights forced cooperation among firms that had been competitors, and groups of large manufacturing concerns were compelled to form cartels to streamline production. Dividends were held at six percent, and any excess was to be invested in government bonds. Products were to be standardized and priorities set.

In practice, few of these programs yielded the results that were intended. Nazi officials were soon confounded by the very cartels that they had encouraged. Many of the associations learned to reduce party meddling by uniting against its directives. And the chief executives of the prosperous state-affiliated combines connected to the arms industry often found ways to avoid purchasing government bonds, plowing the excess profits back

Huge pictures of German youths overhang an armaments display at a 1937 exhibition in Berlin. Supposed evidence of Germany's growing might, the weapons— a Henschel 123 biplane and a World War I-era heavy artillery piece—actually were obsolete.

into their companies in hopes of reaping even greater returns later on.

The heaviest burdens of the war economy were borne by the German worker. In some respects, that worker was better off than in earlier years, because the buildup had caused an acute labor shortage. A man with a factory job—few women held such jobs in conservative prewar Germany—could be sure of keeping his position, unless of course he happened to be Jewish or otherwise fell into official disfavor. But as the decade wore on, workers discovered that their take-home pay was shrinking and their standard of living declining. The labor unions that might have forced a pay increase had been abolished in 1934. In their place was the government-backed Labor Front. This "organization of creative Germans of brain and fist," as its charter read, was dedicated not to its members' welfare but to the interests of the state. The right to strike was suspended, and wages were set by government decree. As if this were not enough, an ever-larger portion of each paycheck was drained off to pay taxes, Labor Front dues, and exorbitant fees for unemployment and disability insurance. And workers who grew dissatisfied with their jobs often found it difficult or impossible to change positions. Under the Four-Year Plan, skilled metalworkers were forbidden to take new jobs without the approval of their district labor office. Others were kept from moving by their bosses, who held a government-issued workbook for each employee; no worker could apply for a new position unless his employer agreed to surrender that document.

Meanwhile, a barrage of propaganda appeals sought to fire up the hard-pressed populace for "the battle for raw materials." There were scrap-metal drives, victory-garden campaigns, and admonitions to replace dinner-table delicacies with low-priced substitutes. Good Germans switched from meat to fish, from white bread to rye, from butter to margarine. As Joseph Goebbels, minister for information and propaganda, pointed out, "We can do without butter, but despite all our love of peace, not without arms. One cannot shoot with butter, but with guns."

Giving up butter did not solve the problems of the war economy, however. The avalanche of business regulations contributed nothing to managerial efficiency. Nor did the work laws inspire much enthusiasm. In consequence, productivity in German factories, though improved since the depths of the depression, still lagged behind that in the rest of the industrialized world. The resulting backlogs of orders only aggravated the squabbling among the branches of the Wehrmacht; each insisted that its own needs took priority. The army lobbied for more tanks and big guns, more helmets and rifles; the navy pushed for more warships and U-boats; the Luftwaffe could never get enough airplanes. Procurement officers for the three services had to fight one another for every rivet and shell casing.

German soldiers tend a cabbage patch near a concrete blockhouse, part of the fortifications built along the French frontier after 1936. Like other Germans with arable lots, garrison troops were urged to bolster the Reich's shaky food supply by gardening.

It was Göring's job to portion out these resources, but the air minister was never a fair judge of who should get what. Not surprisingly, the Luftwaffe reaped the lion's share. Nearly half of all military spending was funneled in its direction. Yet even under Göring's fatherly care, the Luftwaffe and its suppliers never succeeded in meeting their quotas. In October 1936 General Erhard Milch, Göring's deputy at the Air Ministry, outlined a scheme that called for eighty new models and variations to move into production within the next two years, boosting the Luftwaffe's arsenal to more than 12,000 planes. A year later, however, production problems forced him to reduce the goal by 25 percent.

The designers of the airframes themselves, meanwhile, continued to set standards for the world to follow. Souped-up versions of such revolutionary designs as Willy Messerschmitt's Me 109 fighter and the elegant Do 17 Flying Pencil—so called for its slender configuration—won trophies at airshows all over Europe. But for every success story there were several false starts or outright fiascos, many of them results of the Air Ministry's inability to decide what kind of models it wanted and how to use them. Focke-Wulf expended 3,000 hours of engineering time remodeling its FW 58 trainer to meet the Luftwaffe's shifting specifications, only to be told that just sixty of the planes were needed.

Perhaps matters would have flowed more smoothly if Walther Wever, the Luftwaffe's energetic chief of staff, had been around to channel them. But Wever's death in June of 1936 left Milch and Göring without a navigator to redirect their bureaucratic machine when it strayed off course. Wever's successor, Major General Albert Kesselring, was a good administrator, but he lacked Wever's vision and his grasp of technical matters. Nor did it help that the jovial, freewheeling Ernst Udet stayed on as chief of the Technical Office. The former stunt pilot had shown initiative in pushing the development of a dive bomber for the Luftwaffe, but nothing in his temperament or experience qualified him to judge questions of technology. Udet admitted as much. But Hitler had come to like him, so Udet it was.

The confusion at the Air Ministry was perhaps best exemplified by its inability either to pursue development of a workable long-range bomber or to drop the concept entirely. Before Wever's death deprived the program of its strongest advocate, Göring had already begun to undermine the efforts of his chief of staff. On one occasion, while touring the Junkers factory, Göring was shown a full-scale wooden mock-up of a heavy bomber, the giant four-engine Ju 89. "What on earth is that?" he demanded, flying into a tantrum. "Any major project such as that can be decided only by me personally!" he bellowed, and he stomped out of the hanger. So development of the Ju 89 languished, then ceased entirely. Yet the search for a heavy bomber did not expire with Wever. Dornier had a prototype, the Do 19, ready for a test flight in 1936, only to be told that the craft would have to meet higher performance standards requiring new engines. Work proceeded for another year before the Do 19 joined the Luftwaffe's long list of canceled projects. In the end, the Luftwaffe would make do with medium-range bombers such as the He 111 and the Do 17, which could be made more rapidly and at less expense. "The Führer," Göring confided to an aide, "does not ask me what kind of bombers I have. He wants to know only how many."

The Luftwaffe's problems in design and production, coupled with the larger troubles of the war economy as a whole, might have impelled Hitler to delay or suspend his strategic agenda had it not been for the encouragement he received from events on a distant front. Within a few months of the Rhineland venture, an invitation reached Hitler from Spain that would lift German war planning from the realm of theory. In Spain, German fighting men would learn how to make the best of the tools they were given, and the results would whet Hitler's appetite for conquest.

On the evening of July 25, 1936, Hitler and most of the Nazi hierarchy were in the Bavarian city of Bayreuth, where they had gone to immerse them-

selves in the soaring music and Teutonic legend of Richard Wagner's operas. At the production's final curtain the Führer repaired to the Wagner family villa nearby. Awaiting him were three travel-weary delegates from Spanish Morocco. Two were overseas German businessmen, Nazi party members, and the third was a captain in Spain's newly formed Nationalist air force. They had come to seek the Führer's help.

A week earlier, political tensions in Spain had erupted into civil war. A group of Nationalist generals, alarmed at growing communist influence in Spain's popularly elected Republican government, had attempted to seize power. The rebels already controlled more than a third of the country. But the Republicans held Madrid and also the rich mining and industrial centers along the north and east coasts. To capture these regions, the Nationalists needed more troops—in particular, the crack regiments of Foreign Legion and Moroccan soldiers that were stationed in North Africa under General Francisco Franco. There was just one problem. The Spanish navy, which remained loyal to the government, was patrolling the waters between North Africa and Spain, ready to blast any rebel ships that attempted to cross. Franco had sent the three delegates to Germany in the hope that Hitler would lend him airplanes to effect the transfer.

Powerful figures in Germany were already mulling over events in Spain, and they were wary of becoming entangled there. The Reich's foreign minister, Baron Constantin von Neurath, argued that support for Franco would anger France and England. And top Wehrmacht generals thought such aid would be militarily wasteful, a squandering of resources that Germany badly needed to meet the goals of the Four-Year Plan.

No one knew where Hitler stood. At first, he offered little encouragement to the delegates dispatched by Franco and questioned them pointedly about the general's prospects for success. But then, one of the delegates recalled, the Führer voiced his concern about the "danger of the Red peril overwhelming Europe." That was the clue. Franco was asking for ten transport planes. Hitler offered twenty, along with an escort of six fighters. The transports would be Ju 52s, the type of dependable trimotor passenger craft that Hitler himself flew in. No need to worry about money, he said. Payment could be worked out later. Undoubtedly, the Führer was thinking of tapping Spain's rich deposits of iron ore.

Hitler then called in Göring and War Minister Blomberg and informed them of his decision in the presence of the three delegates. Blomberg, who opposed the aid, maintained a discreet silence, but the volatile Göring complained petulantly about the risks involved, only to withdraw his objection when he realized that Hitler was adamant; Göring later claimed that he recognized the proposed airlift as a rare opportunity "to test my

◁ **World War I ace Ernst Udet wore many hats in the burgeoning Luftwaffe. In the photograph at top left, he indulges his first love, skimming the ground while doing aerobatics at a 1932 airshow near Berlin. At top right, in a picture apparently signed by Willy Messerschmitt, technical director Udet listens as the brilliant, overbearing designer expounds a point while tugging Udet's uniform sleeve. In the bottom picture, Udet poses with Ernst Heinkel before setting a speed record in Heinkel's experimental fighter, the He 100.**

young Luftwaffe." Escorting the delegates to the door, Hitler closed the fateful meeting with a message for the man who sent them: "Give General Franco my best wishes for the defeat of communism."

So began Operation Magic Fire, code-named for a circle of fire that the Wagnerian hero Siegfried penetrates to rescue the captive Brunhild. The operation would begin in secrecy, for Hitler did not care to directly challenge those western democracies sympathetic to the Republican cause, especially when the fate of the Nationalist revolt was uncertain.

To conduct the sensitive airlift, the Luftwaffe sought out single men such as Lieutenant Hans Trautloft. He was summoned to see his commander at an air base near Cologne a few days after Hitler authorized the operation. The baffled Trautloft was told to pack his bags; he had just "volunteered" for a special mission. Hours later he was on his way to a second base, at Döberitz, where he joined other officers assigned to instruct Franco's pilots in handling the fighters that were being sent to escort the transports. Trautloft and his fellow pilots resigned their commissions, to be classified officially as reserves, and exchanged their uniforms for civilian clothing. Around midnight on July 31 they left Germany as members of an ersatz tour group aboard the steamer *Usaramo*, which had been loaded with 773 crates containing the components of six He 51 fighters and ten Ju 52s. The other Ju 52s, commandeered from Lufthansa, were being flown to Morocco or to Nationalist-controlled Seville to start the airlift. It was a precarious eleven-hour flight. One crew landed by mistake in Republican-held territory, and its members were jailed for several days before the German ambassador, protesting indignantly about the seizure of a commercial aircraft, obtained their release.

By the second week of August, the transportation of men and matériel for the airlift had been completed, and Operation Magic Fire was in full swing. Ju 52s shuttled across the narrows from Morocco to the Spanish mainland, with some pilots making as many as five round trips daily. At times forty or more tough, wiry Moroccan troopers, their flowing djellabahs tucked about their knees, would herd into a stripped-down cabin designed to hold only seventeen passengers; to compound their discomfort, many of the troops became sick in the turbulent air over the strait. By early October 13,000 men had been whisked to Spain, along with roughly 500 tons of ammunition and other equipment, including 36 artillery pieces and 127 machine guns. It was history's first major military airlift.

In the beginning the Germans tried to minimize their presence. The

Twin-engine Heinkels prepare to take off from a field on the Ebro River in northern Spain. Lacking larger planes, the Luftwaffe would rely on these He 111s and similar Ju 88s for heavy bombing in the world war to come.

Junkers transports flew unarmed and with blacked-out markings. The Germans were there to advise and abet, nothing more. But the temptation to enter combat was too strong for some pilots to resist. On August 13, after a few transports drew antiaircraft fire from a Republican cruiser in Málaga Bay, one Luftwaffe pilot jury-rigged a bomb bay in the floor of his Ju 52— a conversion the plane was well suited for—and bombed the offending warship, putting it out of commission for several months.

A short time later the first German fighter pilots entered the fray. By mid-August it had become clear that the plan to hand freshly assembled He 51 fighters to hastily trained Spanish pilots was ill conceived. Since Republican planes offered no effective opposition to the airlift, the biplanes had been diverted to hotly contested battle zones on the mainland, and Franco's brave but inexperienced fliers were paying the price. In the space of a few weeks, four He 51s went down. More warplanes were on the way, but German pilots assigned to advise the Spaniards grew frustrated at the losses and took to the air themselves. On August 25 Hans Trautloft and his Luftwaffe comrade, Lieutenant Kraft Eberhard, each shot down an enemy plane over Spain, registering the first kills in a German tally that would exceed 300 before the civil war ended.

In the first months of German intervention, such exploits were isolated and unauthorized. But by October, when the airlift concluded, Hitler and his generals were prepared to take a more active, if still covert, part in the Spanish conflict. This time Hitler was ready to act without an official request from Franco, because it had become clear to the Führer and his advisers that the war in Spain was more than an ideological struggle—it was a critical proving ground for new weapons and tactics.

To make the most of this opportunity, the Wehrmacht in late October authorized the formation of the Condor Legion. The name was suggested by Göring to signal that the unit's primary mission was to test German prowess in the air. Indeed, the main components of the developing legion were a bomber group, originally comprising four twelve-plane squadrons of converted Ju 52s, and a fighter group, made up of four nine-plane squadrons of He 51s. (As more-advanced fighters and bombers came off the assembly line, they would be rushed to Spain to supplement or replace the original equipment.) In addition, the Condor Legion would include a standard reconnaissance squadron of twelve planes; a reconnaissance-bomber squadron of fourteen seaplanes; a flak group of eight batteries, five of them equipped with the fearsome 88-mm antiaircraft guns forged by Krupp; and separate communications and maintenance groups. Although the Wehrmacht committed no regular ground troops to Spain, four companies—each equipped with twelve lightly armored Panzer I tanks—were attached to the Condor Legion along with a few hundred army advisers commanded by Lieutenant Colonel Wilhelm Ritter von Thoma, a disciple of Heinz Guderian. Unlike the Luftwaffe pilots, who were now authorized to enter combat, the tank personnel were restricted for the most part to a training role, leaving the bulk of the fighting to Franco's tank crews.

Recruitment for the Condor Legion began at once. Soon hundreds of volunteers—willing or otherwise—were following the secret trail pioneered by the recruits for the airlift back in July. Clad in civilian clothes, they boarded merchant ships at Hamburg, Stettin, and Swinemünde. By all appearances they were tourists bound on vacations sponsored by the Nazi party organization Strength through Joy. Stowed below decks, in crates marked "Furniture" and "Christmas Decorations," were rifles, antiaircraft guns, and disassembled warplanes. Once at sea, the vessels headed south

Outside Tangier in November 1936, Moroccan troops board a Ju 52 trimotor to be airlifted to Spain to fight for Franco's Nationalists. The sixty-three Ju 52s that Hitler eventually committed to Franco were useful transports but flawed bombers.

and ran the Republican blockade to Cádiz. From there, the men and matériel moved inland to Seville, the main German base. In time, a combat force of around 5,000 men—serving tours that averaged nine months in length—was assembled in Spain under the command of stocky, monocled Hugo Sperrle. "My most brutal looking general" is how Hitler once described Sperrle. His chief of staff, Wolfram von Richthofen—cousin of the World War I ace—had just left his post as the Luftwaffe's head of research and development. He now had a front-line seat from which to view the German aircraft industry's products in action.

The Condor aviators wore tropical uniforms with Spanish insignia.

Though about to plunge into fierce combat, they regarded their assignment as a lark. New arrivals toured the sights of Seville and Granada, including the Moorish Alhambra with its famous Court of Lions, and marveled at the flamenco dancing of the local gypsies. Some of the recruits' racier diversions were organized with military precision. A Spanish pilot attached to the legion for training recalled how the Germans took their pleasure at Seville's notorious red-light district: "The men were marched up in formation, and if the houses were full, the overflow was lined up in the street, ready to advance in single file on orders from the commander inside."

The Germans were by no means the only foreign presence in Spain, and their numbers were always comparatively small. Franco had petitioned Mussolini for aid also, and the fascist Italian leader responded by sending a ground force that eventually reached 60,000 men. Mussolini also dispatched some bomber and fighter groups—although they would play a less aggressive part than Göring's Luftwaffe.

Foreign aid also flowed to the Republican side. France's socialist government supplied guns and aircraft but no troops. In time, 40,000 volunteers from various countries, including nearly 3,000 Americans and a few thousand anti-Nazi German and Austrian exiles, joined the International Brigades to fight fascism in Spain. But the Republicans' chief source of weapons and skilled men was Soviet Russia. Moscow eventually sent about 1,000 aircraft, 1,500 artillery pieces, and 900 tanks, along with perhaps 2,000 pilots, tank drivers, technicians, instructors, and other specialists.

The Russians made their debut in late October of 1936 as Franco's forces, reinforced by the airlift, closed in for what they expected to be an easy and triumphant assault on the city of Madrid. Four regiments of loyalist professionals stood ready to defend the capital, along with a ragtag army of volunteers from the city's barrios and rural environs. The defenders were short on guns, ammunition, and air support. Just as their situation grew desperate, the first large shipments of Soviet tanks and aircraft reached the capital. Buoyed, the Republicans launched a counterattack and managed to break through the enemy lines south of Madrid, although the Nationalists quickly regrouped.

On November 7 Franco's forces tried again to take Madrid. The city's garrisons, reinforced by soldiers from the International Brigades, dug trenches and gun emplacements and parceled out their meager stores of ammunition. Women and children built barricades of books and household furniture. When a soldier fell, a civilian was there to take up his weapon. A new battle cry rang through the city: *¡No pasarán!*—They shall not pass! The Nationalist offensive soon bogged down.

Above the city, meanwhile, aviators dueled for control of the skies. On

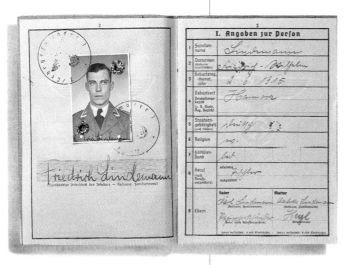

These identity papers belonged to the German pilot Friedrich Lindemann. At top, his Luftwaffe paybook states that he was born in 1915 and joined the air force in 1935. The bottom ID, showing "Federico" Lindemann in civilian clothes, was carried by the pilot when he flew with the Condor Legion in Spain. Lindemann survived the Spanish war but died in the 1940 Battle of Britain.

November 13 Lieutenant Eberhard, who had scored one of the first German kills in August and was now commanding a fighter squadron, took off from his base at Ávila, where a Russian bombing raid two days before had damaged some of his He 51s on the ground. Nearing the Casa de Campo, a contested park on the outskirts of Madrid, Eberhard joined a dogfight and was killed by a bullet through the heart; his Russian adversary managed to parachute from his flaming plane before it crashed, only to descend among a group of angry Spanish civilians who mistook him for a German pilot and kicked him to death.

Frustrated by the capital's resistance, the Nationalists next sought to bomb Madrid into submission. Until now Franco had tried to limit civilian casualties by declaring a large section of the city off-limits to bombers. But on November 18 those restrictions were dropped, and a combined force of Ju 52s, piloted by both German and Spanish crews, and Italian Savoia-Marchetti bombers ravaged the city with 2,000-pound blockbusters. The bombadiers had been ordered to aim at large public buildings, but, lacking sophisticated bombsights, they scattered their cargo far and wide. The bombing soon grew even more haphazard when the raids were switched to nighttime to avoid losses to enemy groundfire. A number of hospitals were hit, and many residential buildings were pulverized. The raids continued until November 22, with the pilots setting their course by the light of burning buildings. For the first time ever, a modern air force had turned its might against a civilian population.

Still Madrid did not give in. More than 1,000 civilians had been killed or wounded, but the carnage only stiffened the resolve of the survivors. Indeed, the raids translated into a major propaganda victory for the Republicans and their supporters abroad. For the Germans, it was a first lesson in the limits of strategic bombing.

His direct assault on the capital stymied, Franco resolved to isolate Madrid with repeated thrusts at its supply routes to the north. One attack in early January at Las Rozas de Madrid, along a major highway, allowed panzer commander Thoma to test Guderian's theories on armor deployment. Both sides in Spain had used tanks as mobile artillery for support of ground troops, dispersing their armor among their infantry regiments.

Thoma, with the backing of Richthofen, planned a coordinated assault in which the German Panzer I tanks would be massed for a breakthrough. The attack would begin with a two-hour artillery barrage, followed by a sweep of He 51s to bomb and strafe key points of resistance. Then the panzers would roll in. The infantry was to march up last, securing the ground the tanks had already taken. Here in essence were the tactics of blitzkrieg.

The attack started in good order, and at first it seemed successful. But the Republicans had a formidable asset in reserve—a squadron of Russian T-26 tanks. Compared with the 5.4-ton panzer, with its thin plating and twin machine guns, the 8.5-ton T-26 boasted thick armor and a 45-mm cannon mounted in a turret that could pivot 360 degrees. Facing such opposition, the panzer crews could yield or be destroyed. Even as the Nationalist forces retreated, however, Thoma knew that the fault was not with his tactics. His panzers were not powerful enough. Thoma offered a reward of 500 pesetas to any soldier who brought him a disabled Russian tank. Soon he had several. Some he kept for future engagements. The others he shipped to Germany for dissection by Krupp's panzer designers.

The failure of the Nationalists to force the surrender of Madrid meant that there would be no quick resolution of the conflict. Fighting would rage across the land for another two years before Franco prevailed. But Spain's ordeal was the Condor Legion's opportunity. Thus far, the German commanders had learned much about the limitations of their arsenal. Now they would have the chance to evolve a formula for victory.

With the Madrid campaign at a stalemate, the Nationalists shifted their attention in early 1937 to the mining communities and industrial centers of Spain's northern coast. This was Basque country—home to a fiercely independent people who supported the Republican government chiefly because it had promised them autonomy. Republican forces in the north were concentrated in the province of Vizcaya behind a fortification system they called the Ring of Iron, which the attackers found all but impregnable. Nationalist general Emilio Mola Vidal, seeking a quick victory to restore morale, decided to resort to air power on a massive scale. "If submission is not immediate," he declared, "I will raze all Vizcaya to the ground, beginning with the industries of war. I have the means to do so." The general's main instrument was the Condor Legion's bomber squadrons.

Those squadrons had been bolstered in recent months by the arrival of thirty new medium bombers—fast twin-engine He 111s, which could carry more than a ton of explosives, and equally swift Do 17s, or Flying Pencils. The new planes arrived none too soon, for the old converted Junkers had turned out to be woefully inadequate. With a top speed of 175 miles per

Germans Who Fought for the Republic

Hundreds of Germans fought on the other side in the Spanish Civil War, joining the Republican army to battle the Hitler-backed Nationalists. Most were communists who had fled Germany when Hitler took over in 1933. The exiles made their way to war-torn Spain and enrolled in the 11th and 12th International Brigades, which were made up of volunteers from seventeen nations, including France, Great Britain, and the United States.

Many of the Germans fought in the Thaelmann Battalion, named in honor of Ernst Thaelmann, leader of the German Communist party; he was arrested after the Reichstag fire and sent to Buchenwald, where he was eventually murdered. The battalion engaged in some of the civil war's most vicious combat, helping to defend Madrid against tanks and bombers operated by fellow Germans. During especially heavy fighting in 1937, the battalion was so depleted that, when ordered to attack, the survivors had to transmit, "Impossible. The Thaelmann Battalion has been destroyed." Nevertheless, the battalion fought in Spain for another year.

Carrying a banner bearing their battalion's name and the communist hammer and sickle, Germans in the Republican army march out to defend the vital Madrid-to-Valencia highway during the bloody winter of 1937.

hour, the Ju 52s had become easy prey for Russian I-15 fighters—powerful, snub-nosed biplanes that could fly up to 220 miles per hour and swoop down on the bombers with four machine guns blazing. Nor could the Ju 52s hope for much protection from the German fighter squadrons, whose He 51s lacked the speed and maneuverability of the I-15s and were being diverted to low-level strafing and bombing runs. To make matters worse for the Ju 52 crews, their plane's trimotor design, with an engine mounted in the nose, meant that they had no guns pointing forward. The new He 111 bombers, by contrast, carried machine guns fore and aft, and like the Flying Pencils, they could outpace the Russian I-15s.

On the last day of March the Condor Legion's reinforced bomber squadrons thundered into action. During the next three weeks, wave after wave of Condor aircraft—He 111s, Do 17s, the remaining Ju 52s, and low-flying He 51s—swept over the Ring of Iron, blasting the defensive lines and the cities they guarded. The major seaport and industrial center of Bilbao was hit every clear day in April. The nearby rail junction at Durango was smashed to rubble. Even less significant targets took terrible punishment.

The market town of Guernica, for instance, contained little of military importance. There was a bank, a candy factory, some churches and small hospitals. Only a few structures could be classed as strategically significant: the railroad station, a small-arms factory on the town's outer edge, and a highway bridge leading east toward Bilbao. But at 4:30 p.m. on April 26, as farmers and traders exchanged their cattle and produce in the central marketplace, the church bell rang, warning of incoming planes. The people headed for cover in cellars, under bridges, and in prepared dugouts. Five minutes later the first He 111 arrived and dropped six heavy bombs.

For the next three hours the Condor warplanes rained destruction upon Guernica. The first strike blew the front off of the Julian Hotel, exposing four floors. About 100 yards away a volunteer fire fighter, Juan Silliaco, was knocked to the ground by the blast. Looking up he saw dismembered arms, legs, and heads flying through the air. In later sorties, the warplanes dropped incendiaries on rows of tightly packed wooden houses, setting off devastating fires. Three hospitals were hit; sick children, wounded soldiers, and the doctors and nurses who attended them died together.

Father Alberto de Onaindía, a Basque priest, took shelter in the woods on the outskirts of town. He saw several He 51s swoop down, their machine guns blazing. They caught other refugees in the open. Mothers, children, grandfathers "were falling in heaps, like flies," Onaindía remembered, "and everywhere we saw lakes of blood." As the bombs fell and Guernica burned, the cloud of smoke and grit rose so thick that the later flights had to come in below 600 feet in order to distinguish the town from the countryside.

German involvement in the Spanish Civil War began in the summer of 1936 with the airlift of General Francisco Franco's Nationalist troops from Spanish Morocco to the mainland. Later that year, German forces aided the Nationalists in an unsuccessful effort to capture Republican-held Madrid. The focus of the fighting then shifted to Spain's north coast, where German air raids around Bilbao crushed Republican resistance. In 1938 the Nationalists and their allies struck out across the northern provinces toward the Mediterranean, eventually enveloping Madrid from the north and east. By mid-March 1939, Franco's forces had fought their way into the ancient capital city.

Its engine warming, a sleek He 112 waits on a Spanish airfield for Boddem to take it up. Heinkel failed to sell the He 112 to the Luftwaffe, which was committed to the Me 109, but Spain bought some, as did Hungary.

Boddem smiles in the cockpit of his Messerschmitt, the plane in which he shot down Russian fighters that were flying for the Republicans.

In a retouched newspaper photograph, French ski troops on an Alpine hillside tend the bodies of crash victims lying a few yards from the wrecked transport in which Boddem was killed.

Willi Boddem's Spanish Cross, in gold with diamonds, was presented posthumously by the German government.

The Untimely End of a Luftwaffe Ace

Among the most admired pilots in Spain was Lieutenant Wilhelm Peter Boddem, the son of a Düsseldorf railroad worker. Described by a fellow German as "small in stature and shy of manner—not your typical fighter pilot," Willi Boddem was nevertheless daring and expert at dogfighting; he shot down ten Russian planes during his two tours of duty with Squadron 134 of the German Condor Legion.

He was also, it turned out, an effective test pilot and salesman for the prickly designer Ernst Heinkel. When Heinkel sent a number of his pet He 112B fighter planes to Spain in 1938, Boddem demonstrated the new aircraft to leaders of the Nationalist air force. The Spaniards purchased all of the He 112s that Heinkel offered.

Ironically, after risking his neck repeatedly in combat, Boddem was killed following his second tour, when the transport returning him to Germany crashed in the French Alps. He was awarded the Spanish Cross, which was given to only twenty-seven Condor Legion airmen. Heinkel wrote a simple tribute: "I will always miss his kind and comradely manner."

At dusk, when the last wave departed, much of Guernica was ablaze. The ruins were still smoldering the following morning when foreign journalists arrived. They found a dazed population sifting through rubble for loved ones and treasured possessions. One correspondent counted 600 bodies laid in a nearby field. The final death toll would never be known; as many as 1,600 people may have perished. The center of town was demolished. A full 70 percent of Guernica's houses were destroyed, another 20 percent were seriously damaged. But the small-arms factory was virtually untouched. The highway bridge remained standing.

Centuries earlier Guernica had been the region's capital, a shrine to the Basque spirit of freedom and independence. Here, at the foot of a venerable oak tree, Spain's monarchs had pledged to respect the rights of the local citizens. The town now became a symbol of war's atrocity. Much of the world press raised a passionate outcry against the Luftwaffe's murderous ways. Publicly, the Germans denied responsibility, claiming that "Red" terrorists had set the town afire. The men of the Condor Legion knew better, however, and few of them cared to boast of the incident. "We did not like discussing Guernica," recalled one fighter pilot.

Whatever the international implications of the Guernica raid, it succeeded in weakening Republican resistance in the area. By early May Nationalist ground forces had swept past the town and were pressing toward Bilbao. The final assault on that city came in mid-June, and it afforded another test for the Condor Legion's panzers. At Bilbao German tank crews saw action alongside the Spaniards they had trained.

One German tank commander later reconstructed his impressions of the

In a terror bombing that outraged the world, the village of Guernica in northern Spain goes up in flames after He 111s pounded it with explosives and incendiaries on April 26, 1937.

Bombs tumble from the bay of an He 111 during a 1939 raid on port installations in Valencia. The plane's defensive armament was limited to light machine guns mounted in the nose, on top of the fuselage, and on a retractable platform in the belly.

assault on the city's outer line of defense—a row of bunkers that were held by Basque mineworkers: "There is no movement we can detect. But we already know that those mineworkers have nerves of steel. We have gotten to within 200 meters of the defense positions, firing away at the dark embrasures. Every hit we score raises some whitish dust that makes the gun ports invisible for a few seconds.

"A dashing Spanish captain is in the lead up ahead. From time to time, he even opens the hatch of his tank to orient himself. Just to remind him to be more careful, I fire a few rounds at the turret of his tank. We have gotten used to this way of conversing with each other. All at once, there is a great deal of noise. The Reds are up on the parapets, throwing hand grenades, mostly at the tracks of our tanks. Others take careful aim at seemingly vulnerable spots on our vehicles. Still others leave their cover and try to urge their comrades on with wild gestures and hoarse cries. At this short range they are picked off the moment we spot them. In some

instances, the cone of fire even sweeps them along for a short stretch.''

That evening the Basques evacuated the line. And on the following day, June 18, the Republicans abandoned Bilbao to the enemy. It was an important victory for the Nationalists but by no means a decisive one. Large areas in the north remained to be secured before Franco could shift his attention to the Republican strongholds along the east coast. In the upcoming campaigns, however, the Nationalists would profit by the expert support of a refurbished Condor Legion fighter group *(pages 166-177).*

By the summer of 1937, the fighter group had received more than thirty Me 109s—early models of the racy monoplane fighter that had gone into production at Messerschmitt's Bavarian plant during the previous autumn. The Me 109s arrived none too soon, because the Soviets were introducing their own high-performance, single-wing fighter to the skies over Spain— the I-16, whose 775-horsepower engine allowed it to reach a top speed of 288 miles per hour, only marginally slower than the Me 109. The Republicans called their fleet new fighters *Moscas,* or flies. To the Nationalists, they were *Ratas,* rats.

At first, the pilots of the Me 109s found the Ratas pesky opponents. But in Germany, Messerschmitt was constantly refining his machine, and in early 1938 a high-powered model of the fighter, with a phenomenal top speed of 323 miles per hour, was dispatched to the Spanish squadrons. Unrivaled now, the Me 109s hungrily patrolled the skies in pairs or in loose

formations of four, their sharklike profiles glinting in the Iberian sun.

Other pilots in the fighter group, meanwhile, were adjusting to a less glamorous role—flying ground support in the He 51s. Few were pleased with the assignment, which they saw as vaguely dishonorable. "Carrying out our orders made us feel like poachers who do not use their weapons decently, as true hunters do," confided Adolf Galland, commander of the legion's Mickey Mouse squadron, whose planes were adorned with a likeness of the Disney cartoon character.

There was nothing trifling about the missions Galland's squadron performed, however. His pilots routinely flew several sorties a day, and their low-level flights were frightening enough. Captain Harro Harder, sent to knock out a Republican gun battery, touched down after returning with every plane in his flight perforated with bullet holes. "The attack lasted only eight minutes," he noted, "but it was a miracle we survived." To reduce the risks, He 51 pilots learned to approach in a line, one close behind the other, so that each successive plane was screened by its predecessor; sometimes the lead pilot would then loop around for another pass, and the trailing planes would follow like the cars on a carousel. Alternately, when the fighters were attacking a broad target such as a line of earthworks, the pilots would approach from the rear, flying side by side, and on signal drop all their bombs at once, creating a neat row of explosions that the Germans dubbed the "little man's bomb carpet." Carpet bombing would one day become a standard tactic of air assault.

With practice, the pilots of the He 51s achieved a high degree of accuracy on such runs. But true pinpoint bombing was possible only with the new Stukas, whose steep angle of descent allowed pilots to target their prey head-on. The first three Ju 87 dive bombers reached Spain in January 1938 and were assigned to the fighter group to supplement the He 51s. The entire arsenal of the fighter group was put to an exacting test in mid-February, when Franco launched the last stage of a campaign to relieve a surrounded Nationalist enclave at Teruel, capital of the eastern province of that name. On February 17 the He 51s and Stukas pounded the enemy's defensive perimeter, punching an opening that Nationalist troops soon exploited. By February 20 Franco's troops were entering Teruel, but the Republicans still stubbornly held a few heavily fortified points, and the Stukas were sent in to pulverize them. The following day, with the Republican escape route cut off, swarms of Ratas suddenly appeared over the town; Me 109s rose to the challenge, shooting down seven Soviet fighters without sustaining a loss.

The taking of Teruel was a prelude to Franco's climactic drive. Over the next twelve months, as Nationalist divisions battled eastward through

This badge, with a skull and crossbones and small tank surrounded by oak leaves, was awarded to favored personnel by the Condor Legion's senior tank commander, Colonel Wilhelm Ritter von Thoma.

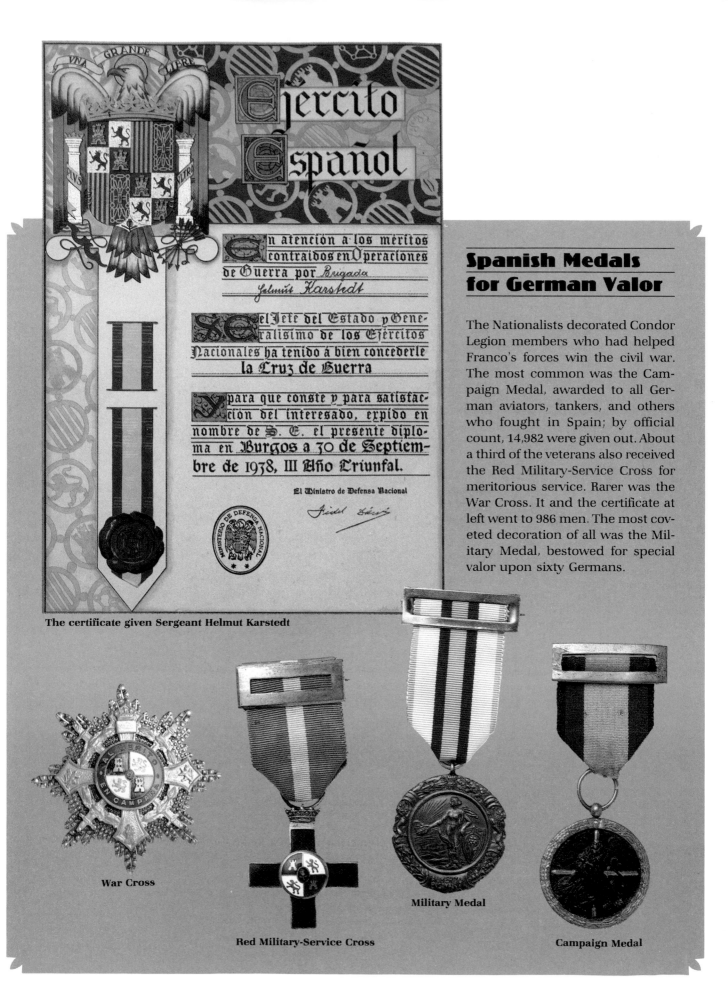

Ejercito Español

En atención á los méritos contraidos en Operaciones de Guerra por *Brigada Helmut Karstedt*

S. E. el Jefe del Estado y Generalísimo de los Ejércitos Nacionales ha tenido á bien concederle **la Cruz de Guerra**

Y para que conste y para satisfacción del interesado, expido en nombre de S. E. el presente diploma en **Burgos** a 30 de Septiembre de 1938, III **Año Triunfal.**

El Ministro de Defensa Nacional

MINISTERIO DE DEFENSA NACIONAL

The certificate given Sergeant Helmut Karstedt

Spanish Medals for German Valor

The Nationalists decorated Condor Legion members who had helped Franco's forces win the civil war. The most common was the Campaign Medal, awarded to all German aviators, tankers, and others who fought in Spain; by official count, 14,982 were given out. About a third of the veterans also received the Red Military-Service Cross for meritorious service. Rarer was the War Cross. It and the certificate at left went to 986 men. The most coveted decoration of all was the Military Medal, bestowed for special valor upon sixty Germans.

War Cross

Red Military-Service Cross

Military Medal

Campaign Medal

Aragon and Catalonia to the Mediterranean, the Condor Legion continued to contribute, refining the blitzkrieg tactics first demonstrated outside Madrid in January of 1937. These assaults were deftly coordinated by Condor Legion commanders and their Spanish counterparts, who occupied posts near the front and were linked by radio to ground and air units. Improved communications—and a better understanding of the capabilities of the weapons in the German arsenal—enabled commanders to respond swiftly and effectively to Republican threats. When the command post learned of the approach of heavy Soviet tanks, for instance, there was no need to commit the vulnerable panzers to a suicidal encounter. Instead, one of the flak group's mobile 88-mm batteries was dispatched to meet the attack with barrels lowered—one of many applications devised in Spain for the big guns. Ultimately, it was not the superiority of German equipment that made the difference in Spain but the ingenuity with which the various instruments of war were orchestrated.

The Soviets, for their part, brought impressive weapons to bear in Spain, but they never achieved the same degree of coordination. By late 1938 they were cutting their losses and withdrawing. In February of 1939 the Republican government evacuated Madrid, and a few weeks later the Nationalists trooped in. For all practical purposes the war was over.

That spring the last representatives of the Condor Legion returned to Berlin. There they marched triumphantly through the Brandenburg Gate along with 10,000 other veterans of the Spanish Civil War who had completed their tours earlier. Göring had tried his Luftwaffe and found it worthy. His newer aircraft were as good as any machines in the world, and his pilots had honed their skills in rigorous combat. His commanders had learned some important lessons: the devastating power of heavy tactical bombardment along the front lines, the value of close coordination between air and ground forces.

The proven doctrines, the battle-tested men, the fine-tuned machines of war—all were now at the disposal of Hitler, who little more than six years earlier had inherited a depressed economy and a discouraged military establishment scarcely able to challenge the weakest of Germany's neighbors. In a few months Hitler would commit the Reich to a war of conquest—a struggle for which the Wehrmacht and the nation as a whole were only partly prepared. But such were the strides made by innovative industrialists and tacticians that the chinks in Germany's armor would scarcely be noticed in the opening act of that fateful drama. On September 1 pilots and tank commanders who had tested their nerves and their skills in Spain would cross into Poland to execute carefully coordinated missions in what one of them called the "miracle of the German blitz." ✚

Flights of the Condors

No element of the Condor Legion played a more dramatic part in the Spanish Civil War than the Luftwaffe's fighter group J/88, shown in action on these pages. If the unit's exploits had been publicized, its pilots would have been toasted as heroes throughout all of Germany. But the work of the fighter group—indeed, of the entire Condor Legion—remained shrouded until the war was almost over.

So quietly was the program carried out that when the first Luftwaffe volunteers embarked for Spain, even fellow pilots were unaware. "We only noticed that one or other of our comrades vanished suddenly," an officer recalled. "After about six months he returned, sunburned and in high spirits. He bought himself a new car and in the greatest secrecy told his more intimate friends the most remarkable stories about Spain."

Those intriguing tales—reinforced by the prospect of combat bonuses and promotions in rank—lured many of Germany's most promising young fighter pilots to aid a rebellion, the issues of which few of them cared about. Any who expected a joyride, however, were soon disabused. Between a pilot's first scramble in the morning (left) and his collapse into a bunk at night, he might fly up to ten sorties. In winter the aviators almost froze in the open cockpits of their He 51 biplanes, returning to base so stiff with cold they had to be lifted from the airplanes and their limbs massaged back to life. In summer, noted squadron leader Adolf Galland, "we flew in bathing trunks, and on returning from a sortie looked more like coal miners, dripping with sweat, smeared with oil, and blackened by gunpowder smoke."

But the experience gained by the fliers proved to be priceless. Those who survived the elements—and the bursts of enemy flak and machine-gun fire—returned to Germany to form the muscle of the Luftwaffe's fighter arm. Their skill at handling some of the world's fastest, most maneuverable warplanes would soon be confirmed on a larger stage.

German ace Harro Harder relaxes with a Luftwaffe comrade of Scottish descent, Douglas Pitcairn (*far left*). Harder painted a swastika on his He 51 (*below*) in defiance of an order banning German insignia on Condor Legion craft. He shot down eleven planes in Spain, one in the He 51 and ten in an Me 109.

Fire consumes an He 51 that crashed in Vitoria, Spain, in September 1936, killing the pilot, Eberhard Hefter. The plane's engine failed as Hefter attempted a stunt at the end of his mission; he thus became the first member of J/88 to die in action.

Making the Best of a Vulnerable Biplane

At first the German fighter group in Spain was equipped exclusively with He 51s (left), which were outgunned and easily outmaneuvered by the best Russian fighters. "Considering the technical inferiority, any gutsiness is senseless," German pilot Harro Harder noted in his diary in 1936. And the commander of the Condor Legion, Hugo Sperrle, reported glumly that He 51 squadrons, far from shielding German bombers as intended, often had to "seek the protection of the bombers' machine guns."

The tables turned dramatically, however, when the swift Me 109 (pages 170-173) took over the escort role and the He 51 was relegated to ground support. Initially, the transition was perilous for the He 51 pilots, who approached targets at such low altitudes that their planes were pierced by splinters from their own bombs. But once the fliers mastered the new role, they developed a grudging fondness for the venerable biplane. Adolf Galland, who returned to Germany in 1938 after flying more than 300 sorties in the same He 51, found it hard to part with his battle-scarred craft: "She had received her baptism of fire and had been riddled by Red antiaircraft fire but had brought me back safely every time."

Mastering the Volatile Messerschmitt

The Messerschmitt's arrival in 1937 gave the Luftwaffe control of the Spanish skies. The sleek Me 109 monoplane, with its enclosed cockpit and liquid-cooled engine, could soar to a height of 30,000 feet and reach a speed of nearly 300 miles per hour, outpacing all opposition.

The power of the Me 109 made it skittish in turns, and its narrow landing gear proved tricky *(below)*. But German aces such as Werner Mölders *(opposite)* were undeterred. "Today was great," he wrote in his journal on July 25, 1938, after leading his squadron into a melee that pitted twenty-seven Messerschmitts against forty Soviet fighters. "All the Me's entered the circus up there, diving into the hornet's nest now and again." The Russians felt the sting, losing four planes while the German squadrons landed intact—a pattern that had become familiar to Franco's foes.

Werner Mölders *(right, before canopy)* confers with a crewman who is about to load a machine gun located in the wing of Mölders's Me 109. In four months Mölders scored fourteen *Luftsiege*, or air victories—a record for the fighter group. Later a new pilot evidently registered a fifteenth kill in the same Messerschmitt, adding another stripe to the running tally on the plane's tail *(above)*.

◁ Ground personnel check the
underside of an Me 109 after it
flipped on landing at Alar del
Rey in northern Spain. The pilot,
Reinhard Seiler, escaped
with minor injuries and went
on to notch nine kills.

Bridging Gaps in Language and Culture

Limited by their fuel supply to flights of two hours, the pilots of J/88 flew an average of three sorties a day, relying on their ground crews to repair, refuel, and rearm the planes quickly. Most mechanics knew the planes intimately, having assembled them from components shipped in crates from Germany. During lulls, crewmen and pilots worked to refine the planes and experiment with new devices, such as the firebomb at right.

Many mechanics were Spanish, which created communication problems. Some Germans resorted to tourist phrase books—or tried snatches of their schoolboy Latin—to bridge the language gap. And Franco's insistence that the Spaniards attend church on Sundays whenever possible deprived pilots of help while tinkering on the Sabbath. But whatever the snags, fliers valued their crews and found small ways to express their gratitude: Pilots who scored a kill often were awarded a case of German beer, which they were quick to share with the men who kept them flying.

A crew member of the Top Hat squadron checks out a gunsight on an Me 109 *(above)*, whose tail has been propped up so its weapons can be aimed horizontally. Machine guns were the fighters' principal armament, and they demanded constant maintenance *(left)*, since a nine-plane squadron might fire 25,000 rounds in a day. The He 51 also served as a bomber, and mechanics devised a deadly use for its auxiliary fuel tank *(right)*; they girded it with two small fragmentation bombs that exploded when the tank was dropped on a target, spewing flaming gas in every direction.

The Dive Bomber's Terrifying Debut

Success with low-level bombing earned the fighter group a special assignment in January 1938: It was to test a powerful warplane that would leave its mark on history—the Ju 87 dive bomber, known as the Stuka. By late 1938 the German bomber group in Spain would have its own Stukas, but the first three-plane squadron was entrusted to experienced fighter pilots. Their emblem was a pig, the German good-luck symbol, which they named Jolanthe (*top right*). The Stukas' targets included hard-to-hit bridges and crossroads (*right*). Like a bird of prey, the pilot made a high approach, then swooped toward his objective with sirens wailing—which terrified defenders below.

The pioneering sorties of the tiny Jolanthe squadron were deemed successful, and in 1939 German factories rolled out 557 Stukas.

A Stuka pilot over Spain makes a dizzying descent on a target *(left)* in a photograph taken by the plane's gunner. The Stuka *(below)* had a 640-horsepower engine that enabled it to carry a crew of two and a 550-pound bomb, or a pilot and a 1,100-pound bomb.

Dive bombing let the pilot approach his objective head-on and target it with unprecedented accuracy. In March of 1938 a Stuka scored a near bull's-eye on a crossroads at Alcalá de Obispo *(below)*. One road remained open, but traffic on the other was halted until workers cleared a path around the crater.

Uncorked champagne signals a day's combat well done as fighter-squadron members unwind at an airfield near La Cenia. By

the civil war's end, all of J/88 had cause to celebrate: The group had recorded 313 kills and lost only 26 pilots.

Acknowledgments

The editors thank the following individuals:
England: Dorset—David Fletcher, Royal Armoured Corps Museum. London—Andrew Mollo. Surrey—Brian Leigh Davis. Federal Republic of Germany: Babenhausen—Heinz Nowarra. Berlin—Heidi Klein, Bildarchiv Preussischer Kulturbesitz; Gabrielle Kohler-Gallei, Archiv für Kunst und Geschichte; Wolfgang Streubel, Ullstein Bilderdienst. Cologne—Marge Hünerbach,

Lufthansa Public Relations. Koblenz—Meinrad Nilges, Bundesarchiv. Mainz—Karl Ries. Munich—Hans Ebert, Messerschmitt-Bölkow-Blohm; Elisabeth Heidt, Süddeutscher Verlag Bilderdienst; Heinrich Hoffmann; Gerhard Patt, Director of Public Relations, Dornier. Stuttgart—Sabine Oppenländer, Bibliothek für Zeitgeschichte; Professor Dr. Jürgen Rohwer, Bibliothek für Zeitgeschichte. Waiblingen—Werner Haupt.

Wuppertal—Jost W. Schneider. France: Paris—Cécile Coutin, Conservateur, Musée des Deux Guerres Mondiales; Christophe Thomas, Direction des Status et de l'Information, Ministere des Anciens Combattants. German Democratic Republic: Berlin—Hannes Quaschinsky, ADN Zentralbild. Italy: Rome—Gabriella di Ciaula and Massimo Scioscioli, Istituto di Studi per la Storia del Movimento Repubblicano.

Picture Credits

Credits for the illustrations from left to right are separated by semicolons, from top to bottom by dashes.
Cover: Heinrich Hoffmann, LIFE Magazine, © Time Inc. 4, 5: UPI/Bettmann Newsphotos. 6-9: Ullstein Bilderdienst, West Berlin. 10, 11: UPI/Bettmann Newsphotos. 12: Jean-Loup Charmet, Paris. 15: Map by R. R. Donnelley and Sons Company, Cartographic Services. 18, 19: Imperial War Museum, London. 21: Bildarchiv Preussischer Kulturbesitz, West Berlin. 22, 23: Bundesarchiv, Koblenz. 24: Larry Sherer, Library of Congress, from *Unsere Reichswehr*, copyright 1932 Neufeld and Henius, Berlin. 25: AP/Wide World Photos. 26, 27: Heinz Nowarra, Babenhausen—Bundesarchiv, Koblenz (2). 29: Fried. Krupp GmbH, Essen. 30: Süddeutscher Verlag Bilderdienst, Munich. 33: From *The U-boat*, by Eberhard Rossler, Arms and Armour Press, London, 1981. 34: Topham Picture Library, Edenbridge. 35: Popperfoto, London—Bildarchiv Preussischer Kulturbesitz, West Berlin. 36, 37: Süddeutscher Verlag Bilderdienst, Munich. 38: From *Deutsche Flugzeugführerschulen und Ihre Maschinen, 1919-1945*, by Karl Ries, Motorbuch Verlag, Stuttgart, 1988—Heinz Nowarra, Babenhausen—Karl Ries, Mainz-Finthen. 39: Ullstein Bilderdienst, West Berlin. 41: Heinz Nowarra, Babenhausen. 43: MBB, Munich. 45: Süddeutscher Verlag Bilderdienst, Munich. 46, 47: UPI/Bettmann Newsphotos. 48, 49: Larry Sherer, Library of Congress, from *Unsere Reichswehr*, copyright 1932 Neufeld and Henius, Berlin. 50, 51: Margaret Bourke-White, courtesy Margaret Bourke-White estate—Süddeutscher Verlag Bilderdienst, Munich. 52: Ullstein Bilderdienst, West Berlin. 55: Archiv für Kunst und Geschichte, West Berlin. 57: Süddeutscher Verlag Bilderdienst, Munich. 58, 59: Heinrich Hoffmann/Bildarchiv Preussischer Kulturbe-

sitz, West Berlin. 61: UPI/Bettmann Newsphotos. 62: Mary Evans Picture Library, London. 65: Süddeutscher Verlag Bilderdienst, Munich. 66, 67: AP/Wide World Photos. 69: Süddeutscher Verlag Bilderdienst, Munich. 70, 71: Archiv für Kunst und Geschichte, West Berlin. 73: UPI/Bettmann Newsphotos. 74: Second World War Study and Research Centre, Brussels. 77: Margaret Bourke-White, courtesy Margaret Bourke-White estate. 78-81: Süddeutscher Verlag Bilderdienst, Munich. 82: National Archives, no. 242-HB-1165A5. 84, 85: Larry Sherer, uniforms courtesy Roger Hall, daggers and helmet courtesy Edward Owen. Background, Library of Congress. 86, 87: Larry Sherer, uniforms courtesy George A. Petersen, daggers and helmet courtesy Edward Owen. Background, Bildarchiv Preussischer Kulturbesitz, West Berlin. 88, 89: Larry Sherer, uniforms courtesy Richard Mundhenk, daggers courtesy Edward Owen. Background, National Archives, no. 306-NT-129OF-12. 90: Bildarchiv Preussischer Kulturbesitz, West Berlin. 92, 93: UPI/Bettmann Newsphotos; John Scott, courtesy USAF Historical Research Center. 94: Keystone, Paris. 95: Larry Sherer, courtesy George A. Petersen. 97: Bundesarchiv, Koblenz. 98: Karl Ries, Mainz-Finthen—Keystone, Paris. 100, 101: Bundesarchiv, Koblenz. 102: Ullstein Bilderdienst, West Berlin. 105: Bildarchiv Preussischer Kulturbesitz, West Berlin. 106, 107: Bildarchiv Preussischer Kulturbesitz, West Berlin. 108: Andrew Mollo Collection, London (copyright Historical Research Unit). 110, 111: Art by John Batchelor. 112: Ullstein Bilderdienst, West Berlin. 113: UPI/Bettmann Newsphotos. 114: Süddeutscher Verlag Bilderdienst, Munich. 116, 117: Copyright Aerospace Publishing, Ltd., London/Weapons Museum, School of Infantry,

Warminster—Larry Sherer, courtesy U.S. Marine Corps Air-Ground Museum, Quantico; Larry Sherer, courtesy Bureau of Alcohol, Tobacco and Firearms (2). 118, 119: Süddeutscher Verlag Bilderdienst, Munich—from *Mein Wechselvolles Leben*, by Karl Dönitz, Musterschmidt-Verlag, Göttingen, 1968. 120: Bibliothek für Zeitgeschichte, Stuttgart. 121: National Archives, no. 306-NT-1290B-14. 122, 123: National Archives, no. 306-NT-110-103. 124-131: Library of Congress. 132: Hugo Jaeger, LIFE Magazine, © Time Inc. 135: Ullstein Bilderdienst, West Berlin. 138: AP/Wide World Photos. 140, 141: National Archives, no. 306-NT-863G-1. 143-145: Süddeutscher Verlag Bilderdienst, Munich. 146: AP/Wide World Photos; John Scott, courtesy USAF Historical Research Center—Lufthansa Public Relations, Cologne. 148: Karl Ries, Mainz-Finthen. 149: Süddeutscher Verlag Bilderdienst, Munich. 151: Karl Ries, Mainz-Finthen. 153: Larry Sherer, courtesy George A. Petersen. 155: David "Chim" Seymour/Magnum. 157: Map by R. R. Donnelley and Sons Company, Cartographic Services. 158, 159: Larry Sherer, courtesy George A. Petersen, except lower left, Karl Ries, Mainz-Finthen. 160: © G. D. Hackett. 161: Ullstein Bilderdienst, West Berlin—© G. D. Hackett. 162: Larry Sherer, courtesy George A. Petersen, from *Die Wehrmacht* (Sonderheft), May 30, 1939. 163, 164: Larry Sherer, courtesy George A. Petersen. 166, 167: Larry Sherer, courtesy George A. Petersen, from *Die Wehrmacht* (Sonderheft), May 30, 1939. 168, 169: Karl Ries, Mainz-Finthen. 170, 171: Karl Ries, Mainz-Finthen, except upper left, Larry Sherer, courtesy George A. Petersen, from *Der Adler*, May 31, 1931. 172, 173: Karl Ries, Mainz-Finthen. 174, 175: Ullstein Bilderdienst, West Berlin; Karl Ries, Mainz-Finthen (2). 176, 177: Karl Ries, Mainz-Finthen.

Bibliography

Books

Angolia, John R., and Adolf Schlicht, *Uniforms & Traditions of the German Army, 1933-1945.* 3 vols. San Jose, Calif.: R. James Bender, 1984-1987.

Batty, Peter, *The House of Krupp.* New York: Stein and Day, 1967.

Bender, Roger James, *The Luftwaffe.* Mountain View, Calif.: R. James Bender, 1972.

Bender, Roger James, and Warren W. Odegard, *Uniforms, Organization and History of the Panzertruppe.* San Jose, Calif.: R. James Bender, 1980.

Borkin, Joseph, *The Crime and Punishment of I. G. Farben.* New York: Free Press, 1978.

Burden, Hamilton T., *The Nuremberg Party Rallies, 1923-39.* New York: Praeger, 1967.

Carr, William, et al, *Hitler's War Machine.* London: Salamander Books, 1976.

Cooper, Matthew, *The German Army, 1933-1945.* London: Macdonald and Jane's, 1978.

Craig, Gordon A.:
The Politics of the Prussian Army, 1640-1945. London: Oxford Univ. Press, 1964.
War, Politics, and Diplomacy. New York: Praeger, 1966.

Davis, Brian Leigh, *Badges and Insignia of the Third Reich, 1933-1945.* Poole, England: Blandford, 1983.

Deist, Wilhelm, *The Wehrmacht and German Rearmament.* Toronto: Univ. of Toronto Press, 1981.

Deist, Wilhelm, ed., *The German Military in the Age of Total War.* Leamington, England: Berg, 1985.

Doenitz, Karl, *Memoirs.* Transl. by R. H. Stevens. Cleveland: World, 1959.

Elson, Robert T., and the Editors of Time-Life Books, *Prelude to War* (World War II series). Alexandria, Va.: Time-Life Books, 1977.

Elstob, Peter, *Condor Legion.* New York: Ballantine Books, 1973.

Erlam, Denys, *Ranks and Uniforms of the German Army, Navy and Air Force.* London: Seeley Service, 1940.

Fest, Joachim C.:
Hitler. Transl. by Richard Winston and Clara Winston. New York: Harcourt Brace Jovanovich, 1974.
The Face of the Third Reich. Transl. by Michael Bullock. New York: Pantheon Books, 1970.

Galland, Adolf, *The First and the Last.* Transl. by Mervyn Savill. London: Eyre Methuen, 1973.

Garriga, Ramon, *La Legion Condor.* Madrid: G. Del Toro, 1975.

Gordon, Harold J., Jr., *The Reichswehr and the German Republic, 1919-1926.* Princeton, N.J.: Princeton Univ. Press, 1957.

Goerlitz, Walter, *History of the German General Staff, 1657-1945.* Transl. by Brian Battershaw. New York: Praeger, 1954.

Guderian, Heinz, *Panzer Leader.* Transl. by Constantine FitzGibbon. Washington, D.C.: Zenger, 1979.

Hart, B. H. Liddell, *The Other Side of the Hill.* London: Cassell, 1973.

Heinkel, Ernst, *Stormy Life.* Ed. by Jürgen Thorwald. New York: E. P. Dutton, 1956.

Hidalgo Salazar, Ramon, *La Ayuda Alemana a España, 1936-1939.* Madrid: Librería Editorial San Martin, 1975.

Homze, Edward L., *Arming the Luftwaffe.* Lincoln: Univ. of Nebraska Press, 1976.

Irving, David, *The Rise and Fall of the Luftwaffe.* Boston: Little, Brown, 1974.

Klein, Burton H., *Germany's Economic Preparations for War.* Cambridge, Mass.: Harvard Univ. Press, 1959.

The Luftwaffe, by the Editors of Time-Life Books (The Epic of Flight series). Alexandria, Va.: Time-Life Books, 1982.

Macksey, Kenneth J.:
Guderian: Creator of the Blitzkrieg. New York: Stein and Day, 1976.
The Tank Pioneers. London: Jane's, 1981.

Manchester, William, *The Arms of Krupp, 1587-1968.* Boston: Little, Brown, 1968.

Mason, Herbert Molloy, Jr., *The Rise of the Luftwaffe.* New York: Dial Press, 1973.

Mosley, Leonard, *The Reich Marshal.* Garden City, N.Y.: Doubleday, 1974.

Noakes, J., and G. Pridham, eds., *State, Economy and Society, 1933-39.* Vol. 2 of *Nazism, 1919-1945.* Exeter, England: Univ. of Exeter, 1984.

Nowarra, Heinz J., *Die Verbotenen Flugzeuge, 1921-1935.* Stuttgart: Motorbuch, 1980.

O'Neill, Robert J., *The German Army and the Nazi Party, 1933-1939.* New York: James H. Heineman, 1966.

Overy, R. J., *The Nazi Economic Recovery, 1932-1938.* London: Macmillan, 1982.

Padfield, Peter, *Dönitz: The Last Führer.* New York: Harper and Row, 1984.

Proctor, Raymond L., *Hitler's Luftwaffe in the Spanish Civil War.* Westport, Conn.: Greenwood Press, 1983.

Ries, Karl, *Deutsche Flugzeugführerschulen und Ihre Maschinen, 1919-1945.* Stuttgart: Motorbuch, 1988.

Ries, Karl, and Hans Ring, *Legion Condor, 1936-1939.* Mainz: Dieter Hoffmann, 1980.

Robertson, E. M., *Hitler's Pre-War Policy and Military Plans, 1933-1939.* New York: Citadel Press, 1967.

Rössler, Eberhard, *The U-boat.* Transl. by Harold Erenberg. London: Arms and Armour, 1981.

Salas Larrazabal, Jesus, *Air War over Spain.* Ed. by David Mondey, transl. by Margaret A. Kelley. London: Ian Allan, 1974.

Shirer, William L.:
Berlin Diary: The Journal of a Foreign Correspondent, 1934-1941. New York: Knopf, 1941.
The Rise and Fall of the Third Reich. New York: Fawcett Crest, 1962.

Shores, Christopher, *Las Fuerzas Aereas en la Guerra Civil Española.* Transl. by Guillermo Solana. Madrid: Editorial San Martin, 1977.

Showell, Jak P. Mallmann, *The German Navy in World War Two.* Annapolis, Md.: Naval Institute Press, 1979.

Smith, W. H. B., and Joseph E. Smith, *Small Arms of the World.* Harrisburg, Pa.: The Stackpole Co., 1962.

Snyder, Louis L., *Encyclopedia of the Third Reich.* New York: McGraw-Hill, 1976.

Southworth, Herbert Rutledge, *Guernica! Guernica!* Berkeley: Univ. of California Press, 1977.

Stachura, Peter D., ed., *The Nazi Machtergreifung.* London: George Allen and Unwin, 1983.

Taylor, Telford, *Sword and Swastika.* New York: Simon and Schuster, 1952.

Thomas, Hugh, *The Spanish Civil War.* New York: Harper and Row, 1977.

Wheeler-Bennett, John W., *The Nemesis of Power.* London: Macmillan, 1964.

Wyden, Peter H., *The Passionate War.* New York: Simon and Schuster, 1983.

Wykes, Alan, *The Nuremberg Rallies.* New York: Ballantine Books, 1970.

Periodicals

Birchall, Frederick T., "Hitler Shuts Door of Europe to Reds." *New York Times,* September 14, 1937.

Boeninger, Hildegard, "Hitler and the German Generals, 1934-1938." *Journal of Central European Affairs,* April 1954.

"Germany." *Time,* March 16, 1933.

Guilmartin, John F., Jr., "Aspects of Airpower in the Spanish Civil War." *The Airpower Historian,* April 1962.

Kuh, Frederick, "Germany's Reichswehr." *Fortune,* January 1933.

Meier, Hans Justus, "Rohrbach." In *Beiträge zur Geschichte.* Bremen: VFW-Fokker, 1974.

Oberkommando der Wehrmacht, *Wir Kämpften in Spanien.* Special issue of *Die Wehrmacht.*

Reichsluftfahrtministerium, *Legion Condor an die Front! Deutsche Freiwillige Kämpften für Spanien.* Special issue of *Der Adler,* May 31, 1939.

von Scheele, " 'Legion Condor': Als Erste Freiwillige nach Spanien." *Die Wehrmacht,* June 7, 1939.

Index